SLEEPY

Michael J Rossano

ISBN: 1512183601
ISBN 13: 9781512183603

DEDICATION

For Sylvia

ACKNOWLEDGMENTS

Angelica Guzman who edited SLEEPY.

Sam Gallo who created the front and back covers for the book.

Jimmy Olvera who was there for me all these years but more importantly to help me through the rollercoaster ride of SLEEPY.

My kids who accepted, didn't judge, showed compassion, love and honesty. I'm so proud of you guys.

Jay Franklin who was my partner in crime at work and who inspired me taught me and supported me as we worked our caseloads …Thanks Frankie.

CJ supervisor, mentor, jefe, and friend. I couldn't be who I am dealing and working with kids and families to this day if not for the knowledge, direction and guidance you gave. I will always hold the highest respect for you and will always honor you.

And Lastly, My wife-

You've been supportive of everything I've done. You have always been the best thing to ever happen to me. You are a great wife, loving person and best friend. Thank You for being there and working with me to offer SLEEPY a better life. I will always honor you till the end.

INTRODUCTION

The events you are about to read are a true story about a girl and her family and the rollercoaster of life she goes on. The years will pass as you read and you will see and feel the choices made. The gang lifestyle and the fight for survival are real and the never-ending quest to overcome challenges is real. Sleepy's life will take you through drugs, family dysfunction, hard times, and self-inflicted pain. You will be exposed to the steps taken and interventions used in order to not only change her life, but to save her. This was written for one reason and one reason only – so that YOU, the reader, will hopefully see and understand Sleepy's pain and that her sacrifices may be your success. The goal is that you learn from Sleepy's experiences and that you may grow and be productive, and most importantly, LIVE.

CHAPTER 1

IN THE BEGINNING

The alarm went off, the shower turned on, "Another day" I said to myself. "another day of work, another day of headaches, and another day of hectic trying to help these kids out, but another day of possible success as well."

Today was an important day though, and as I woke I felt more optimism for the day rather than agonizing what would the day bring. I kissed my wife goodbye, made sure the kids were off to school, and prepared myself for my 'other world'.

Arriving at the center on time, anxious to receive my next case; I couldn't control the thoughts in my mind as I walked into the office. Who will be my new case? This was always challenging to me as an Outreach Worker, meeting new cases, developing a plan of action, and watching their attempts to succeed in that plan. It was our goal as a gang intervention program to "decrease the violence involving gangs through Outreach Services." The gang program had just finished its first of a five year grant when I was hired. The model was designed to send workers on the street to work and monitor gang members on a daily basis. We provided assistance and direction and we utilized referrals as needed. Typical referrals would be made to internal programs, outside programs, and specific related professional services.

I pulled up a chair as the meeting was about to begin and we began discussing the assigned cases for each worker. They each were pleased with their assignments and now it was my turn. I was handed a file that had been the topic of discussion for a while now… the file that many workers hadn't wanted to be assigned. This case was going to be a challenge for me, I knew that. I was still the "new kid on the block," but I was up for any challenge, or let's just say, I always had an optimistic attitude.

She was fourteen years old and her moniker on the streets was "Sleepy." The meeting ended at 8:30 A.M. The staff and my supervisor wished me luck as I set off to meet Sleepy for the first time.

It was approximately nine in the morning when I showed up at her home. I stood outside and waited patiently. It was quiet to the point that I could hear myself breathing. My eyes scanned the area. A dog sat in the corner of the yard, tied to a short chain, and I saw a three-foot patch of bare dirt in front of the doghouse. It was the only place the dog was able to walk and he must have paced it a thousand times to make it look that way. The yard wasn't bad but the grass needed mowing. The house was a bit old and I could just imagine the tales it could tell.

I have always felt that the appearance of a person's car, house, dog, and yard could give you a pretty good idea of what you were about to encounter. The neighborhood was low-income. The yards weren't kept up, and most lawns were yellow and tall. There were occasional houses that were maintained, displayed green grass, and clean block walls, although I could still see the barrios gang name tagged or sprayed beneath the more recently painted surfaces of the walls.

I felt bad as I observed an elderly gentleman who lived four houses down attempt to cover yet another gang tagging. The feeling of what this man must go through to keep his home clean was evident. His desire was not to give in, and he obviously constantly continued to cover the graffiti, as neighbors and gangsters looked on. Trying to understand this man only created images of ants and roaches and weeds overrunning your life despite all efforts. It would take a lot more than paint or insecticide to clean up this place. I didn't ask this man... but I'll bet he was confronted by one of the members of the gang because he painted over their name. [Intimidation is one thing all gangs have in common.] This man appeared to be pretty stubborn and didn't stop for one second. I noticed an American flag displayed on his house, and he gave me the impression, because of his tidiness and organization, that he was probably a veteran of the armed forces. He had his pride and stood tall. It even made more sense why the neighborhood street gangs didn't sway him from his mission and why he stood so tall when members walked by. It was a little comical at first, but then after thinking about it, he was probably messed with all the time by gang members and being as proud as he was, he didn't give in to threats or tagging and continued to fight for his dignity and survival. It was something to admire. I wondered if he knew how serious the gang problem really was. I should have gone over and talked to him.

I decided to knock on Sleepy's door. After several times, a child opened the door. She then went back inside and told someone, who I assumed was Sleepy's mother that someone was at the door. A woman in baggy clothes with her hair pulled back in a ponytail came to the door. Looking me straight in the eye, she asked, "Can I help you?"

"Yes," I replied. "I am from the gang project and I'm here to see your daughter."

""I'll get her, but she's still sleeping." She responded.

With that, I knew she was Sleepy's mother. As she walked away, I returned to my truck and waited. My mind took off as I was re-membering the look the mother gave me. It was the kind of look that makes you uncomfortable inside and gives your eyes a sting that you just want to disappear. It was my job to be there, but wasn't so sure they wanted me there.

Understanding how different cultures operate was very helpful in this kind of job. Gaining trust was going to be an issue and I knew not to ask to enter the home because that had been my first contact with them. They didn't know me or what I was about. I didn't expect them to just open the door and let me into their lives. I waited patiently by my truck.

The Hispanic gang culture is very protective and tight-lipped. It is very difficult to develop a trust and respect with someone they don't know. It is the way they have been raised for generations. You must show great patience and speak from your heart when dealing with them because they can somehow see right through those that don't care. I showed Sleepy's mother and their home the respect they demanded by informing them I would wait outside. I sat there for about twenty minutes.

Sleepy finally came out and approached me beside my truck. She looked horrible, with mangy hair and baggy pants that dragged as she walked. She held her head straight down and squinted with the sunlight in her eyes. She looked up and her face told many stories. Her eyebrows had been shaved off and penciled on. She looked tired as if she had been up all night. She looked much older and more experienced than any fourteen year old should. I was surprised to see that this was the "bad girl" that had been discussed in probation and the center over the last week. I don't know what I expected her to look like, maybe just younger. I had difficulty thinking of the right things to say because her appearance had thrown me off my initial plan.

"Hello, my name is Mike and I'm here to help you." I carried on and told her she was the talk of the probation meeting and that she was thought to be out of control and her mom couldn't handle her.

She looked up at me and instead of responding back, she just yawned as if to say, "Yea, hurry up and get on with it. I'm tired and I could care less what you say or think."

After that so-called response, I knew I had a lot of work ahead and this lifestyle was going to take years to turn around.

Sleepy had prison written all over her. She certainly was not your average fourteen year old. Most girls that age don't fight, do drugs, or run the streets with a gang while committing violent crimes. You could tell that life was tough on this kid and she didn't care about her appearance or what anyone thought about her. It appeared she didn't care about anything except her homeboys and homegirls in the gang.

"I just want you to care," I said to her at last. I have always felt that if a person cared, good things would happen. Her response was the same- a yawn. I told her I would see her soon and I left.

After looking through her file, I knew it would be hard to help this girl. Sleepy was an active gang member, doing drugs, angry at the world, and didn't care about much. She had been placed on probation and referred to our program for stabbing another girl. Sleepy's sister took the fall for this and was placed on probation and went into placement for seven months. Sleepy was hardcore and mean. I had my work cut out for me. I believed, although she had anger in her, most of her behavior was a result of learned behavior, as she grew up around this lifestyle watching her brothers and sisters and how they acted in the neighborhood. She had made a name for herself and the ball just kept on rolling down the negative path of life.

Over the next couple of weeks, I stopped by Sleepy's house enough to get a feel for her family and her situation at home. It seemed as though problems started when Sleepy was just nine years old. Dad had gotten hooked on heroin and began to beat up on Mom. Mom got tired of the abuse and filed for divorce. Sleepy blamed Mom for breaking up the family, and then the payback attitude and hatred started.

Sleepy had a large family of four sisters and one brother. Her brother "Midnight" was an OG (Old Gangster) from the hood. He did at least six years in the pen from his involvement with drugs and gangs. Her four sisters had minimal to medium involvement in the gang lifestyle, but understood it nonetheless. None of her sisters or her brother graduated high school. Most of Sleepy's family was on government aid and housing 9 and still is to this day). Sleepy's older sister Maria was at least trying to break away from this type of traditional lifestyle. (I will talk more about her later). Mostly I had seen no change in their lifestyle, just different places to live. Sleepy didn't have the greatest role models while growing up, plus she had resentment toward Mom. At her young age, she had thought Dad was just fine and that Mom caused all the problems. In all my contacts with Sleepy's mother, I perceived her to love Sleepy, but was always preoccupied with her own personal drama and issues. It appeared that Sleepy was never her first priority. I knew Sleepy was too young and immature and out of control to fully grasp the whole family dysfunction, the role of her mother and the inadequacies of her father. Sleepy also didn't recognize or care to recognize the dangers of gangs, the use of drugs, and committing crimes.

I must say there was love in this family, though. They helped each other out and acknowledged each other as family. They just didn't have jobs or do anything to improve their lives. They partied, stayed up all night, and slept most of the day.

I have been around long enough now to see one of the sisters become pregnant, keep the baby and then receive public assistance. The older sisters had also done this and the generations just continue in the same mode. The reality is that people who work in my occupation with intervention and probation will be dealing with children with the same struggles and morals because no one will step up to the plate and make a change. My fight is not only to save this one individual, but to change a generation. Sleepy is just the beginning because once you start building a relationship, you are then working with the entire family. With this family, I didn't need any other kid on my caseload. I would have more than enough work and challenges.

Sometimes on my drive home, I would be sitting in traffic thinking about Sleepy and her family. The first thought that came to mind was Dad and the role of any father. It was evident that something had happened through the years with this father. His job should have been raising and guiding his family. As I have already said, it was evident that Sleepy's father dropped the ball somewhere along the line. As they always say, anyone can be a dad but it takes work to be a father. The only positive I can offer you if you find yourself in a fatherless situation is to first recognize the problem and then start caring for yourself. Basically, if you don't have a father to kick your butt and keep you on track, you need to hold yourself accountable and kick your own butt.

CHAPTER 2

ACTION PLANS/ROLES

Like any case I received, I had to come up with a plan of action on how to assist and guide the client. There were short term goals and also long term goals. Sleepy needed the whole shebang. I was going to throw everything at her and see if these traditional methods of working with at-risk youth would work. Throughout the course of the first two years of working with Sleepy, she would go through several programs and components such as: Anger Management, Culture Diversity, Gang Intervention-Prevention, Individual Counseling, Family Therapy, Job Development, Drug Counseling, Conflict Resolution, Community Service, and other related services.

All of these components were offered to each client but were also a part of Terms and Conditions of Probation. It was common to speak with several PO's on a weekly basis that was monitoring their ward's activities. It was more of the Outreach Worker's job to help clients go through the process. We would guide, direct, and refer clients to each component. We would also provide transportation and sit with them in the class if need be. This to me was the biggest difference between traditional intervention and the gang program. If you took a hundred kids and told them they needed to complete the components by a certain date, most of them would fail, and for obvious reasons; they wouldn't know where to go, they wouldn't have transportation, they didn't feel good. They would not go because they don't care and they would rather get high on weed. However, assign them an Outreach Worker to introduce the desired plan and guide and direct and push and pull and sit in class and work with the family and, and, and, and, and, you get the point.

We drove up to the building where the Anger Management classes were to be held. I had Sleepy and two other kids. My other two partners arrived with their clients from other areas in the city. We all entered the classroom and others present were the Anger Management teacher, three Outreach Workers, and ten gang members from several different gangs. At first you could slice the tension in the room with a knife. The first twenty to thirty minutes were establishing the rules and the class were declared a "safe zone"; no banging or fighting, no drug use or inappropriate behavior.

Class went fairly well, but we did encounter several problems. These kids were all involved in gangs, mostly generational, and now they were forced into one room and made to talk to one another (This would not have been easy for productive kids who did the right things and had family support). We encouraged the kids to speak their minds and then we moved on. Even if the discussions didn't end peacefully, the kids had to agree to not fight in class. Outreach would then meet separately with the individuals involved and attempt to persuade them to let it go.

The Outreach motto is "Pick up a pen, not a pistol", and was created by my supervisor, CJ, who is one of the smartest men I know. I know this Anger Management class saved lives. The instructor was a man named Denny. He was great with kids and knew how to relate to them. He really cared about them. The Outreach Workers and even the Supervisor of the gang program would attend Denny's classes. It wasn't the information that helped the kids the most, it was the teacher.

Sleepy attended Anger Management with Denny most of the time, but her participation was limited. Her focus was always on other things. One afternoon after the class, Sleepy appeared upset and I confronted her. She said that another girl was looking at her. This loss of focus continued to be a challenge for Sleepy. When she did focus and participate in the class, she did very well and she learned. But those classes were few and far between.

One of the first steps Sleepy needed to do was to get back into school. I picked her up to re-register for community school. Sleepy was signed up and given a schedule of Monday through Friday, 7:30am to 11:30am. The level of work she was expected to do was simple and she could work at her own pace. I already knew that the first challenge would be getting her to school on time, since she was a night owl. Sleepy did OK at first, but it was like pulling teeth the whole time. Sleepy didn't care and put forth no effort and would probably take that attitude all the way to Juvenile Hall. Most of the Probation and school staff would tell me to just let her go to jail, or why was I always helping her when she didn't care. These comments didn't surprise me because they were obvious and typical. I let them go in one ear and out the other. It was my job and desire to make Sleepy care.

After several weeks of Sleepy attending school, I became comfortable with the teachers and school staff. They would notify me if Sleepy wasn't at school and it soon became a routine of my pager lighting up twice a week for her no-show at school. One morning after one of these pages, I went to Sleepy's house and she was still wearing the clothes from the night before. Sleepy always wore baggy Levis and a shirt that sported the number 13 on it. The 13 represented the thirteenth letter of the alphabet, "m", which stands for marijuana, also Mexican Mafia. This jersey is common with Hispanic gangs. I tried to talk to her and even threatened her with probation. Sleepy looked at me and did one of her typical yawns. She didn't care and wasn't going to do anything she didn't want to do.

I would continue to try to talk to her, and her mother also tried, but it fell on deaf ears. Sleepy would just call us stupid and tell us to go to hell. She had a terrible attitude and at times I could have just strangled her, but I knew I had to be patient. I just couldn't understand her reasons for her actions and her responses when I confronted her.

The more time I put into trying to understand Sleepy, the more intrigued I became. What had angered this girl so much? I knew she was angry at her mother and probably blamed her for the breakup with her father. It was easy to recognize the family dysfunction and negative role models but there had to be more to it. Was it all her gang's fault, the negative peers, the conversations held in some backyard every night? This aggression and hatred had developed over years. It was embedded in her heart and was beginning to invade her soul. It seemed too big a task to change her behavior but I stayed optimistic and blamed adolescence. I hoped for a brighter future for her as she matured.

I worked daily to assist Sleepy in the plan of actions listed. She had been in the program almost six months and I had established a good rapport with her. I believed she was more comfortable with me; trust and respect were growing. However, she struggled most of the time creating more problems with her attitude. She violated her terms and conditions of probation by using drugs, failing to attend school, and failing to call her PO. She basically drove me up a freaken wall, but I wouldn't give up. I knew if I did, she would just use that as another excuse to keep doing the things she was doing. I knew I had to keep applying the pressure. I was working on a relationship with Sleepy that was based on trust and respect. Only time and perseverance on my part was going to gain this.

Dealing with the gang lifestyle and her attitude were the toughest issues to deal with.

The roles of gang members are very important and have always played together like an orchestra or ball team. In this book, I will be referring to the Hispanic gang culture unless otherwise specified. The male member has many duties. He may fight the enemy which usually represents a different neighborhood. He will protect his turf or territory until death. He will direct younger members to "put in work" or commit a crime. He usually has access to drugs, money, and weapons as needed.

Weapons are usually held by the female members of the click, which is another word for gang. They will stash weapons, carry them, and even lure the enemy in for the purpose of a beat down by their gang. The female members also give themselves to the gang for sex. It is not uncommon for one girl to be with several members of the gang over a period of time. The term for this on the streets is "hood rat." In experiences that I have encountered, the female members are more ruthless, more cunning, and have less remorse for their victims. They also carry weapons more often than the males.

Sleepy fit right into this category. She was mean and cared about her hood or gang more than anything else. Today's female gang member carries as much respect from the gang as a male, and plays a major role in the hierarchy of the gang.

To implement a plan of action with a person like Sleepy is not an easy thing to do. It takes planning and footwork. You must build a circle or network around the individual with other people and agencies in order for it to work. It takes a lot of time to meet with people, set up appointments, and inform them about objectives and their role in your plan. After this is established, then the daily tracking occurs. You are involved with every aspect of the minor's life, socially, educationally, and legally. You are the most important link in collaborating efforts in monitoring one person.

This work doesn't really have a time frame. My pager would go off at six in the morning or ten at night. It's not uncommon to get these pages at all hours. This type of kid is in crisis needs support even when it's not convenient. We set up the initial plan with Sleepy and took it one day at a time.

Sleepy was ready for Juvi when I met her, but Probation granted me some time since I had just started working with her. Sleepy didn't take advantage of any of the help and just kept goofing off. She would miss several days of school and tested dirty or positive for marijuana. It was only a matter of time that Probation would lock her up. They did speak about locking her up at the weekly meetings I attended. I attempted to stall efforts of Probation, but Sleepy wouldn't listen to me. She never respected her Conditions of Probation, so they locked her ass up.

JUVI TIME

Nothing seemed to work with this kid. There were others on the caseload receiving the same attention and assistance and they were responding and doing well. Sleepy had one way of thinking – her way. This way of thinking only meant she would have to pay the hard way. After working with Sleepy for a while now, I realized she was more ingrained into the gang lifestyle than I thought. Sleepy was a complex kid with several emotions going on and she appeared confused at times.

I continued to gather information on Sleepy and I contacted her in Juvenile Hall. I sat on the bench in the middle of the quad area and waited for her. She came out of the closed area with chains and handcuffs on. Her shorts and shirt were bright pink and looked too big for her. She dragged her feet as she walked and looked even more pathetic than the first time I met her, if you can imagine that. I told her she looked like an idiot and asked her several times if this was the kind of life she wanted for herself. Sleepy was used to being in charge and never listening to anyone, but my contact with her that day was just the opposite. I needed to take her power away from her, so I insulted her. I also talked to her about probation rules inside Juvi and how she must listen or else. I told her to tell the staff to kiss her ass the same way she told her mother and see what happens. I confronted her sour attitude, her mean spirited comments. I called her a stupid idiot several times. It honestly felt good because she deserved it. I reminded Sleepy of her current lifestyle and explained the reasons why she needed to listen. I told her she wasn't in charge of shit and from now on I would be telling her what to do and when to do it. Sleepy just stared at me like I wasn't there. At least she didn't yawn so I know she was listening. Then I told her to get her ugly stank-ass-pink- clothes-wearing criminal ass up and go back to the cell with the other inmates. I finished with, "Oh yea, Sleepy, don't forget to talk shit to the Probation staff."

Sleepy was only doing fifteen days, so I needed to be hard on her. It hurt me a little to be like that, but I had to. If I didn't get on her, she would have taken the situation and me lightly and attempt to run all over me. I remember the expression on her face when I yelled at her to go back to her cell. She looked puzzled and hadn't expected that from me. I kept a straight and called the guard to take her back to her cell. Sleepy said that she could talk longer, but I told her I was done talking to her. As she got up and walked away, I looked at her and said, "Hate me now, Love me later." As I walked out of Juvenile Hall, I laughed at myself. Where did I come up with that stupid comment anyway? With Sleepy it will probably be "Hate me now, hate me later."

I know that contact sounds a bit harsh, but at fourteen years old, Sleepy didn't respect anyone and she acted as if she was in charge of everything. I felt I had to take her down a couple of notches. I visited her one last time in the hall. We set a tentative game plan for after her fifteen days in the hall was completed. Sleepy just nodded her head and shrugged her shoulders.

14

I continued telling her, "Hate me now, love me later." She knew I wouldn't allow any disrespect. It was part of her terms and conditions of probation to take part in the Outreach Program and it was my job to keep working with her regardless of what she did. The components that Sleepy participated in were only the beginning. I had to go back to the basics with this girl. The basics meaning words like – appreciation, gratitude, kindness, compassion, respect, caring, hope, dreams, etc., etc. I would take her home sometimes and buy her a burger and fries before dropping her off and she would get out of my truck and just close the door. She wouldn't thank me for the ride or the food, she would just leave. I would then get out of my truck and stop her in her tracks and explain to her the importance of some of those words mentioned above. After this confrontation, she would mutter a half-hearted thank you and go into her house. Hello patience and tolerance again.

I enjoyed going to work every day. I actually couldn't wait to work with the kids and looked forward to the ongoing and never-ending saga with Sleepy. Many kids on the caseload, including Sleepy, have potential and talent but it hardly ever surfaces. Their lifestyle holds them down and any hope is crushed and then we are stuck with a kid who doesn't care. How do you not say "thank you" when someone helps you? It should come as naturally as buttering your toast or pouring syrup on your pancakes. It's just that simple, but yet I found myself having to teach this girl, or better yet, force this girl to be respectful and considerate.

It's easy to identify with Sleepy's anger, isn't it? It's also easy to feel like you know her. If you find yourself sharing some of these feelings, there are things that can be done. At this point, Sleepy didn't care about Anger Management or abiding by her terms and conditions of probation. Her participation in the program was limited and her attitude was horrible. What if she did care? What if Sleepy did well in Anger Management and followed her terms and had a better attitude? Couldn't things be better? Regardless of life's challenges, isn't it easy to know the impacts of caring versus non-caring? The funny thing is we all know what happens when we don't care and we give up and say, "Screw it." We don't have a clue what could happen on the other end, now do we? The challenge as I see it is not with Sleepy's life and the struggles that come with it. The challenge is Sleepy herself.

CHAPTER 3

BACK HOME

S leepy was back at home. Immediate contact with her and re-introducing the plan of action needed to be established. I went to her house and knocked on the door and someone yelled that she would be right out. I heard that Sleepy had a brother who had just finished six years in prison and was out on parole. I didn't know him, hadn't met him, and didn't know where he was staying. After waiting a couple of minutes for Sleepy, a man came out of the house and walked right up to me. As he approached me, I figured out rather quickly that this was her brother. He stood about 5'10", weighed about 180 pounds and went by the name of "Midnight". He wore a muscle shirt, long shorts that covered his knees, and sported tattoos. He reminded me of a tough Indian warrior representing his tribe and confronting the cowboy eye to eye.

At first I was intimidated, but then I realized that because I was helping his sister; I should be accepted and my goal was to keep his sister safe and maybe help his family. I knew respect mattered more now than any other time. He stared at me with eyes that appeared to be very dark. He introduced himself and told me he had heard about me trying to help his sister. I told him that I cared about Sleepy and that I wanted to help her. He said that

Sleepy wouldn't listen and he was sometimes forced to slap her. I told Midnight that I had heard about his slapping from his mother, but it appeared not to help because she continued to screw up.

I then reversed things with Midnight and asked him, "What about when she does good things? Do you pat her on the back and tell her 'Good job'?"

He replied "No."

Then I asked, "Have you ever told your sister that you loved her?" There was a long pause and I told myself, "Oh, crap! Too much, too fast. Now he's mad. Here I am asking him personal stuff he must already feel guilty about. I'm such an idiot."

After a couple of minutes I noticed a tear running down his cheek as he replied, "No." This tear moved me more than I can ever tell you. I realized that although there had been pain and suffering in this family, in some crazy dysfunctional way, there was love. Midnight definitely loved his sister but they were two different people, years apart and he hadn't been there for her. He wanted to be the brother that a sister listened to and could look up to. However, the listening he received from them was out of fear, not love or respect. I understood him and felt his pain and I felt helpless when I spoke to him.

Midnight simply stated, "We are a dysfunctional family who needs help." He turned and walked to the house to get Sleepy.

That was my first meeting with Midnight. I felt I had had a great contact with him and trust and respect had been achieved. I knew as soon as he began to approach me, I needed to gain some respect from him. If he didn't respect me or feel my heart wasn't in the right place it would be the beginning of the end as a counselor in gangs. Well, in that neighborhood, anyway. I would have been shut off in that area. He would have put the word out in the barrio to stay away from me. You see, Midnight was considered an OG (Old gangster). An OG in the hood carries a lot of respect. All he would have to say is that I was an undercover cop or I was with Probation instead of Outreach and I would be done, finished, clocked out.

The human brain is a complex and powerful tool. On his five step approach to me, my brain flashed an "oh shit" warning that I needed to win him over. I knew it was going to happen, but just not then. I was glad it was over and looked forward to our next encounter.

At the time I didn't realize how much I would need Midnight to help me. Sleepy would take off at times and I couldn't locate her and I would go to Midnight and he would find her for me. He would find her alright and she would argue and disobey his wishes and commands and then he would slap her a few times and drag her back home. Sleepy would be pissed at everyone. Her mom, her brother and now me. It was never her fault, the little princess never did anything wrong. There would be many more contacts with Sleepy's bro and more slapping, I'm sure. Sleepy finally came outside and was surprised that I had talked to Midnight for so long. The first thing I said to her was "How was Juvi?" Sleepy smiled and said, "It wasn't so bad." I thought to myself," If you think Juvenile Hall is OK you have problems."

I have found that kids like Sleepy do well in lock-up. There is structure and direction and discipline which are what they lack. Wards get a shower and three meals a day plus a snack. For some, it is better than being at home. Wards are clean from drugs and are able to focus on specifics like school and hygiene. I know some Wards who don't want to leave. Yes, I'm serious, they were afraid to leave. This wasn't Sleepy though…she wanted out.

I was hopeful that the little princess hated Juvi. I hoped she would conform to some of the rules and terms of her probation for fear of being returned to the Hall. I knew she was smart enough, I just wasn't sure she cared. I told her the first thing we would do is write up another plan of action. The only problem was, I was more enthused than she was. I was still in the process of building rapport with this kid so I did what any Outreach Worker would do... I took Sleepy to McDonald's. I learned very quickly that some chicken nuggets, a cheeseburger, and fries with a Sprite worked wonders. We talked about her life over lunch. We talked about drugs, gangs, her family and school. We talked about attitude and desire and goals. I even shared my dad's theory of "if you lay down with dogs, you get fleas", meaning if you stay away from the hood and its members, you wouldn't get into trouble. I was so intense about helping Sleepy because she was such an underdog.

There were two things I liked about Sleepy. Intelligence was one, even though every move she made you thought you were dealing with an idiot. The other was toughness and let's face it, if a kid like Sleepy is going to make it, she would need to be tough. I knew I couldn't force feed a whole different lifestyle down her throat and gradual change was needed, but give me some damn desire or caring. Give me some freaken effort at this instead of yawns and shoulder shrugs. It wasn't easy to work with her attitude and outlook on life, but McDonald's made it a little easier.

My job was to show Sleepy the lifestyle she was living was wrong and it was going to lead straight to incarceration or death. When kids like Sleepy are raised in this sewer thinking and negative lifestyle, you can't tell them it's wrong, or their family is wrong or their gang is going to get them killed. You just need to show them other things that life has to offer and assist them in the change-over. Let's talk ice cream for a minute here. Let's say chocolate is the only ice cream Sleepy ever had. You don't tell her there are dozens of different flavors available. You take her to Thirty-One Flavors and let her see for herself and make her own choice. That's the concept, to show her other ways of life.

Most gangsters don't have a clue beyond their own street or hood or even city. Talking to a kid who has never been to the mountains, played in the snow, or viewed the ocean is not uncommon. Poverty, lack of transportation, drug use, dysfunctional family situations, minimal generational growth, all play a role in why and how this could happen. The traditional family day at the lake is non-existent for kids like Sleepy. It's more like, kick it in the back yard of Dopey's house and smoke out. They have been groomed by the streets, their gang, and their family. How they view life, work, school, and their future is different from the normal child growing up.

Sleepy's sister once had a birthday party for her daughter in their backyard. They had the niece invite all her friends over for the night. They bought her a keg of beer and hired a D.J. to celebrate the occasion. Sounds pretty innocent, huh? Well, the birthday girl was only fourteen years old. Yes, she was allowed to drink too, because she was at home. That made it all O.K. This is the kind of warped parental thinking I am talking about, teaching their kids all the wrong morals. Then the gangs step in and the ball starts rolling. Next thing you know, you have a yawning fourteen year old in baggy pants, walking out the door in gang colors and numbers, who is on probation and hates the world. Their lifestyle is like a sputtering flashlight that stays on sometimes, but you can't count on it to stay on and lead you out of this nightmare you are in.

There is a separate belief of guidelines and rules for kids like Sleepy. The cops are considered the enemy, not a helpful friend. Growing up, their families were involved in illegal activities and had occurrences with the law. Sleepy and other kids like her viewed the cops in a negative way because every time they had contact with the law, it was for a negative reason. They saw mom cry or brother arrested again or one of their homies shot. They literally grew up hating the cops because they were taught to hate. In fact it's their job to hate.

This entrenched layer of misguided beliefs and undisciplined behavior is difficult to deal with. Sleepy and I would be driving down a street and when we would pass a cop, Sleepy would say "fucking pig". I would look over at her and tell her to be quiet and then remind her of what the streets would be like if it wasn't' for the "fucking pigs". I just didn't know if I could change her thinking. Like I said, I just kept showing Sleepy other things and kept working at it. Can I have two scoops, one pistachio and one cookies and cream please?

Hey gangster Sleepy, can you hear me? It's me, Mike. I'm trying to wake you up but you are not listening. I keep trying all my little tricks that I've learned over the years and I am striking out. I know you are smart. I know you can hear me. I know you can understand and carry on a conversation. You are just not listening. Let me see your arms, did you cut your arms again? Sweetheart, we will get through this together. Please don't cut yourself anymore. You are just going through a tough time and I promise it will get better. If you take it one day at a time and work hard, go to school, and stay off drugs your life will be better. You can improve your life no matter how messed up it is by taking one day at a time and doing good on that day. It can happen, I've seen it. Hey, Sleepy, can you hear me? I'm talking to you. Stop yawning. Que estas hacienda, Sleepy? You need to get on the right track, girl. You need to be serious about your actions and your future. I don't want to be getting those calls from prison with you crying and confused about why your life is the way it is. I know your intentions are to not go there, but your actions tell a whole other story. Stop now! Check yourself and get on track. Check yourself now and get on track.

Questions concerning how young Sleepy is and if she is mature enough to make the changes that are necessary continued to ruffle through my thoughts. Sleepy's relationship with her mom is turbulent and her niece Selena, who lives with them, absorbs everything that is going on. Selena seems to be a nice 12 year old little kid with a good attitude and she has respect for others. I was worried that she would learn Sleepy's ways and create problems as she grew older. Looking at Selena reminded me of my garden. I planted carrots and at first you could see a couple of skinny frail green sprigs of the carrot breaking through the ground and then a day later there was a row of sprigs. That's the way I looked at Selena. She didn't ask to break ground but here she is and she'll probably take some farming as well.

CHAPTER 4

BACK TO THE BASICS

S leepy was released from the hall in the middle of the week. I believe it was Wednesday or Thursday when she got out. She didn't want to start school until that following Monday. I didn't know why she felt she deserved a couple of days off, but that was her position so I lined up several other things like components and talking to school counselors and so on. I knew there would be instances when she would want to do things her way, something that was wrong or just didn't make sense. This was one of those times, but we actually got a lot done and scheduled her for several programs, including school. I had to ease my beliefs and show extreme patience with Sleepy. I knew she was going to give me plenty of opportunity to drop her or have probation lock her up. I also made a decision that I wouldn't give up on Sleepy. It was a commitment that I made to myself with only God as my witness. That was it.

I had always heard and had to deal with negative remarks when it came to Sleepy. Probation staff, school staff, component instructors, program outreach workers, all stated the same things. "Sleepy will never do the right thing" or "She's going to prison" or "Give other kids your time, she doesn't care." It was difficult to hear these people talk about her like that. It was even more difficult to defend her.

Sleepy did make me look like a fool, but I expected that. I expected all the comments even though I had a hard time dealing with it. I would set up classes for her to attend and I would inform probation, which was always in the wings to lock her up. Sleepy wouldn't attend; she'd just blow it off. I remember I would catch up to her and she would say things like, "Oh that was yesterday?" I hated that part of her and wanted to give her a "Midnight "slapping more than once. Sleepy just wanted to do her thing. She wanted to run the streets, do drugs, drink, and stay out all night. Sleepy wanted to kick it in the hood and not conform to the workings of society. I told her to be prepared for a clean start on Monday and explained my expectations to her one more time.

Sunday night came and I was anxious to start the next day with the kid. I had set up an appointment for community school and the plan was to pick her up first thing in the morning and start the new process. I arrived at her house Monday morning and picked up Sleepy and her mother.

Sleepy complained all the way there, she wouldn't shut up. She was saying "This school sucks" and "Why can't I go back to the other school?"

I just told her, "This is the school you are going to and that's final. The other school doesn't want you back."

Sleepy got mad and was quiet and wouldn't say a word. I just laughed and that made her even madder. We arrived at the school and spoke to the staff working and we registered her for school.

I then took both Sleepy and her mother out to eat and we talked about a short term goal and a brief plan for the next two weeks. Sleepy was to start school the next day and she was to call me right when she arrived home. This was a daily requirement that I wanted her to do. Working with Sleepy was like being on the ocean with a life vest just keeping you above water, floating along toward land and the next minute...SHARK!

I was truly excited for Sleepy. I thought, "OK, she can do this. She looks good, she is focused, and she is ready for change. She is ready for the scary success that will come from all her hard work and effort. She is ready to finally use her potential and show all those non-believers what she can really do."

It was now Tuesday. Morning turned into afternoon and I impatiently waited for Sleepy to page me. I couldn't wait to hear how the first day of school went. I could hardly stay focused on anything else. I knew I could have called her to find out where she was, but that wasn't the plan. Sleepy needed to step it up and I believed in her. Two hours passed since school had ended for the day, so instead of calling her, I called the school hoping to catch someone still there. Her teacher happened to answer the phone and told me what I didn't want to hear. Sleepy didn't show up for her first day of school and no one even called in. I wasn't disappointed in Sleepy, I was pissed! I was beyond furious and wanted to strangle the little shit. Who in the hell did this girl think she was? How could she not show up? I cursed all the way to her house and trotted up to the front door.

Sleepy's mom came to the door when she heard my truck roar up. Before I could even say a word she told me that Sleepy hadn't come home the night before. I just turned and started back to my truck. I was about to enter the truck when Midnight came walking up, yelling "What's up?"

I told him about his sister, and Midnight said he would find her and have her call me. He was angry when I told him that Sleepy didn't even go to school, didn't even try. I knew he would find her and probably slap her around. I didn't care at the moment, but I later calmed down and thought things between Sleepy and me were about to get worse, not better.

Midnight would find Sleepy, slap her, make her call me crying, and she wouldn't want to talk to me at all, great, just great. Like those effing sharks. Her efforts were poor and although a slapping from her brother wasn't going to help, it was going to happen, like it or not. It was a mixed bag on this one. On one hand, I was glad I told him, knowing he was going to slap her around, and on the other hand it really didn't help at all and would probably make things worse. The only problem was he found her almost every time he looked for her. I felt I had said my piece with Midnight and if he wanted to slap her or not, it wasn't my business to tell him otherwise.

A couple of hours passed and my pager went off and I knew it was her. Sleepy would always page me and leave her number plus 411 or 13. 411 was the info number we all use and you already know what 13 means. I called her back and sure enough, she was crying and pissed. Sleepy was the one who had blown off school, blown off probation, but her mom and I were the jerks. I asked her why she was crying and she told me that Midnight had found her at a hood hangout and slapped her in front of everybody. He then threatened other boys there and told them if she screwed up again, the person she was with was going to pay big time. I attempted to get an intelligent response from her on why she didn't go to school, but she could barely talk. I told her to make sure to attend the next day and things would get better. Sleepy just mumbled, "OK" and then she hung up.

I felt beaten and confused. Why was it so hard for her to abide by the rules? It was like three hundred pound boulders tied to her ankles. I drove home quietly saying to myself, "Go to school Sleepy. Your home girls and that lifestyle will destroy you. This isn't brain surgery, kid, handle your business."

Sleepy stayed home that night. The next morning she told her mother she was headed for school, but she never made it. The school contacted me and informed me of her no-show once again. They told me they would have to drop her if she missed one more day. I told them to just drop her from school and I informed probation to pick her up and place her in the hall again. Probation quickly found her and locked her up. The plan had faltered. The plan didn't even make it a week.

Other clients on my caseload were improving and doing OK. Sleepy had the worst attitude of them all. I didn't know what it was that intrigued me about this girl. Sleepy was a true underdog with issues and a big challenge ahead of her. I felt she had a good chance and had potential, but what would she do?

Most kids I dealt with had two things in common. One – they didn't appreciate their freedom, and two – they didn't value their lives. Value is a strong word. It is what they lacked, it's what Sleepy lacked. I knew I couldn't give up on her and I knew if she didn't respect me, I wasn't going to be able to teach her anything. The plan was to earn respect and trust would follow. Lots of luck.

Sleepy was to appear in court three days late on a violation of probation. It was the same violation as before. The main two violations were failure to attend school and positive, or dirty, for marijuana. I attended her court hearing attempting to show this kid some support. The judge talked to her about her recent re-lease from Juvi and her quick return. He also talked about the possibility of an out-of-home placement if she didn't improve and follow some simple instructions. The judge ordered another fif-teen days in Juvenile Hall and for the first time acknowledged me in the back of the courtroom. The judge knew about the special program Sleepy was in and told her to listen more to the guy in the back of the courtroom.

After her hearing, I arranged through her attorney to speak to her. I waited in the small side room of the courthouse. There was a small bench to sit on and a phone on the wall. It was separated from another room by a thick sheet of Plexiglas. The door in the other room opened and Sleepy came in. She was wearing an or-ange jumpsuit and was handcuffed to a chain that went around her waist. Her ankles were cuffed as well. She pigeon-toed her way into the room and sat down. She picked up the phone. I told her how much better her life would be if she cared and just tried to do well. Sleepy looked sad and scared. I was afraid for her. It was at that moment that I realized that I couldn't save her, she had to save herself. I told her I would talk to her mom and the school and see what else could be done when she was released. She walked out with two court officers, her chains clanging, to the van that went back to Juvenile Hall.

I was upset and angry walking out of the courthouse that day. I was upset because her efforts to change were very poor; I was mad because that damned street life was winning the fight. I felt that I was fighting more than just gang membership, drugs, family dysfunction, and hopelessness. I felt like I was in a tug-o-war with the devil.

I walked to my truck in the parking lot with a different view of Sleepy than I had before. I knew I was overwhelmed but I loved it and took it on with open arms. I vowed to be a force in this girl's life that would stand for goodness and honesty and strength. I prayed to God and asked Him to give me the courage and the patience to deal with this kid. I also asked God to guide Sleepy and make her care.

Hall Time
A week had passed and I decided to visit Sleepy at the hall. She came walking out the locked-down cage looking pathetic, as usual. She had an attitude. I immediately became irritated and let her know it. I told her she looked like an idiot and asked her if she felt like one. Sleepy didn't respond; she just shook her head no. I attempted to engage her in a conversation but she only answered in eyebrow talk and shoulder jargon. (Eyebrow talk is when the penciled on eyebrows go up and down and you already know about the shrug of the shoulders.) I asked her if she was mad at me. She responded, "What do you think?" I told her life wasn't Burger King and she couldn't have it her way. I told her to go back to her

cell with the other inmates. I also told her how disappointed I was in her efforts and if she wanted to be a loser, she could be. I said prison was waiting for her. I then stood up and stormed out of the day area and the front door of the hall. I was so upset with this girl. It killed me that she didn't care or have any hope and what the hell was she mad at me for? She was the one who wouldn't follow the laws of the land, but yet it was never her fault. I don't think so.

Sleepy and I both knew the road to success was going to be hard. Just stopping her from smoking marijuana was going to be hard. Her gang meant a lot to her and that lifestyle was entertaining and care-free. What she needed to learn was that it was all temporary, nothing lasts forever. You get high, your buzz goes away. Nothing in that type of life ever stays, there is no building of anything, and the lifestyle won't allow it. This was why her sister moved so many times. There is and never would be any stability in this kind of life, only drama.

I believed in Sleep. I felt she had the courage and the potential to overcome her challenges. I remained focused to push as far as I could. Sleepy gave me every reason to forget about her and concentrate on other kids, but it's hard to explain why she was so important to me. There had to be more divine powers going on here. God had to play a role in this relationship or maybe it was an ego thing with me. Maybe being in sports as a kid wouldn't allow me to quit. All these thoughts flew around in my mind and drove me crazy at times.

I always thought Sleepy would be that diamond in the rough, but I didn't want to tell her that because her gang insignia was the shape of a diamond with writing around it. I decided to call her a rose in a bed of weeds. I asked God for guidance with this girl and asked Him to sprinkle her with some of His "Miracle Grow."

CHAPTER 5

PLACEMENT TIME

S leepy completed her fifteen days in the hall with ease. You see, Sleepy was considered a regular and she knew the staff. Even though she was a pain in the ass and talked a ton of shit, she was likable. Staff took care of her like she was at Club Med.

In her last hearing, the honorable judge decided to place Sleepy in the Day Treatment Center. The hours at the center were Monday through Friday, 7 A.M. to 12:00 P.M. The best thing about this center was the transportation they provided for the kids. They picked up the kids at their homes and drove them to school. Sleepy was lucky the judge sent her to the center because she could remain at home. The judge also had commented on an out of home placement if the center didn't work. The center had small classrooms and two teachers and an aide to help out. The Probation officer was also nearby in an office for assistance as needed. There was plenty of structure, organization, and professionalism. A psychologist for the kids was always available. It appeared to be just what Sleepy needed. I thought, "O.K. This is good. This place offers a lot and is easy with short school hours. This should work out really well."

Sleepy started the Day Treatment Center as soon as she completed her stay in "Club Med," I mean Juvenile Hall. She had a better attitude and did really well adjusting to the school and the schedule. She liked her teachers and the psychologist and was comfortable with her PO. The days she attended class outnumbered the days that she missed and those days were recognized. The PO would drug test Sleepy every week and every week she was clean. What was going on here? Is the little princess finally taking some strides here? Is she coming around and going to improve her life? I was optimistic as always, but was also surprised at her progress.

I found myself spending more time at Sleepy's house since things were starting to look better. Contacts with school staff were positive and my presence wasn't always necessary because everything seemed OK. But the relationship between Sleepy and her mom was horrible. Sleepy loved her mom, but she was angry with her, didn't respect her and acted out purposely to hurt her. Several times a week I would go to Sleepy's house and speak with them about their relationship and how to improve it. The only problem was, I knew what Sleepy was thinking and feeling but she never told her mom. I knew if things were to improve, they needed to talk and confront each other's feelings and this could lead to a blowout. Well, with Sleepy there was a potential blowout over anything.

One night I received a call from Sleepy's mother. It was nine o'clock and she was very upset with Sleepy. I could hear Sleepy yelling in the background. Mom said Sleepy was out of control and was acting crazy and wouldn't calm down. I had no choice but to drive over there to help out with the mess. I felt sort of responsible because I had encouraged Sleepy to speak out and tell her mom how she felt. I rushed over to the house and walked in on two screaming people. It was difficult for me to calm them down. On one hand I didn't want them to. I wanted all the dirt, all the anger and hidden feelings on the table. I wanted them to understand each other's feelings. On the other hand, if I tried to quiet them they might shut down and clam up and that wouldn't be productive. If I could just control the situation and push and guide them to some understanding.

Sleepy was blowing like Mount St. Helen. She wasn't listening to anyone and most of the time wouldn't even let her mom talk. I intervened when I could. I spoke softly and directly and asked questions to each of them when the need arose. They calmed down a little and continued to talk but the mom made a comment about Sleepy's father and that was it! All talking stopped and an angrier Sleepy stormed out. I never fully understood how Sleepy could protect her dad and why she got so defensive when anything was said about him. I guess as a kid growing up with him had its positive aspects and Sleepy cherished those days in her life.

When I had entered the picture when Sleepy was fourteen, it was a whole different story. I saw a middle-aged man who looked broken down, with very little self-respect, and living from place to place. I saw a man hooked on heroin, doing heroin with his oldest son, yet still trying to carry this persona of one who took care of business around the family. He wanted them to think he was in charge. I had several contacts with him and he had thanked me for being there for his daughter. He later died of an overdose of heroin and alcohol.

I had respected his gratitude, but at the same time I was angry because he had given up, quit life and his family, especially his children, and for that I couldn't forgive him. To me, being a father is the most important thing in my life but to him it was a burden. But, yet, Sleepy always defended him and directed all her hate and anger towards her mother. Her mother may have been overwhelmed at times and was struggling to provide for her family, but she loved Sleepy and she was there for her more than her father had ever been.

A few days went by and Sleepy was a no show at school. Her PO called me to tell me he had located her and brought her back to school. She was tested for drugs and she was found positive for marijuana again. He gave her another chance and didn't lock her up. He too, was hopeful she would take advantage of the opportunity and improve her status.

I spoke with her about school and probation and mom stuff. I told her she had a poor outlook and how she acted like she didn't even. I was disappointed with her but at the same time I was still happy the blowout with her mom had occurred. It had needed to happen and now they understood each other a little better than before. I considered it a "wound cleansing". It will hurt when you clean it out, but it will heal faster and better because it was taken care of. The problem was that all of Sleepy's actions were violations of probation and her PO, who had been patient and supportive, was leaning towards more custody time.

It was difficult for me because for the first time since I had met Sleepy, she had shown some promise and what she could accomplish. I was proud of her at that time and in retrospect I wondered what the outcome would have been had I not pushed Sleepy and her mom into that confrontation to work out their issues. The traditional Sleepy would never have spoken to her mom about her feelings and would never have given so much effort in school. I recognized all these things when I spoke to her but I also warned her that probation would probably lock her up. I tried to state my case for Sleepy to her PO but she had smoked marijuana and probation wouldn't forgive that part of it. They agreed she had improved in some areas, but couldn't overlook that smoking. Probation caught up with Sleepy and escorted her to Juvenile Hall. I again tried to reason with probation, but they no longer had any faith in Sleepy. Like I said before, it was always hard to defend her. I knew Sleepy had skipped school, smoked pot, missed appointments and components and then exhibited a bad attitude when confronted, but I didn't feel the community was at risk, just Sleepy was. I asked the court for more time but was denied. Sleepy's court date was three days later and the judge was not happy to see her. He showed his displeasure in his tone and ordered Sleepy to remain in custody and be in court for sentencing two weeks later. The two weeks flew by and Sleepy was back in court and the judge handed her live-in placement. It was a nine month boot camp style live-in facility. The judge spoke about the discipline and structure there and the drug components. He encouraged Sleepy to work hard at the program and to get her life together. I had only a brief moment to talk to Sleepy before they took her away. I could tell she was surprised at the outcome and a little afraid. Yea, I said surprised. Sleepy was upset about the length of time she would spend there. I was actually sad and happy at the same time. I was happy because she would be monitored more closely and be safer. I was sad because I loved working with her and fighting that everyday challenge. I tried to give her some encouragement by speaking positively about the placement. Her response was only shoulder shrugs and eye-brow jargon. As they took her away, I wondered what the outcome would be for all of this. I struggled for positive thoughts. I didn't know when my next contact with Sleepy would be. Good luck in placement, Sleepy.

Over the next month I worked my caseload and also met with the director of the placement that was assigned to. I informed him of the program and its collaboration with the courts. I asked him for his support as well. I asked for monthly contact with Sleepy and to be notified of any problems. I explained the concept of the program Sleepy was in and how contact with a minor shouldn't stop just because of placement. He was very receptive to the information and was happy to support contact. The placement staff was informed and made aware of Sleepy and the program she was in. I introduced myself to some of them, explained the program, and gave them my card. Some staff members had negative attitudes, but some were very helpful. Sleepy saw me talking to them, and knowing how I was, she knew I was arranging a schedule to see her. Before I left, a staff member opened the door to the wards' quarters and I had a chance to wave a quick goodbye to her. Sleepy smiled with an answering wave. I left.

I visited Sleepy several times throughout her custody. I was also paged by staff when Sleepy was in trouble. Most of our talks consisted of me telling her to respect the staff and follow the guidelines of the placement. It was hilarious when Sleepy approached me in the visiting area. She wore green shorts and a green shirt. I made fun of her, of course, because she never sported shorts in the hood. "Hey white legs, get a tan". It was at this placement center where I began to feel that my relationship with Sleepy began to matter to her. All the court dates, the visits in the hall, components, school issues, neighborhood visits, etc., helped in securing a relationship with this girl. I felt she trusted and respected me more and knew I was serious about being there for her. Sleepy's rollercoaster of life wasn't easy to deal with, but I loved it. Every day was a different experience and with Sleepy I never knew what to expect. She definitely had been a handful to this point. It was always my belief that with unconditional caring, with fair and guided direction, every troubled kid could have a decent future. As I recall, Sleepy had spent her fifteenth birthday in Juvenile Hall and would now spend her sixteenth birthday in placement.

Days were turning to weeks and weeks into months. I knew Sleepy's time in placement would go fast and she would be back at home again. I always imagined her going to school, working part time, and taking care of business. It was something I prayed for, but for whatever reason just hadn't materialized yet.

I set up a field trip for Sleepy through the Director of Placement. We took the kids from the gang program to the Museum of Tolerance. Sleepy sat next to me on the ride over and I felt almost like a dad going on an outing with his daughter. She had a smile on her face most of the day and felt the impact of some of the things she saw at the museum. It was a good day with Sleepy. We even teased her about those shorts she was still sporting. "Hey, Sleepy, ever hear of a razor, hairy gangster?" We enjoyed the museum, had a good lunch, and shared thoughts about life. Sleepy went back to placement and I left there feeling happier than I usually did. I thought if she could only be the kid she was today, every day, there would be no limitations. What she gave me today was what I knew was in there in the beginning.

The big question was how to gain this or achieve consistency with the same attitude and outlook as Sleepy had exhibited the day at the museum. When home troubles, gang or negative peer pressures, drugs and other demonizing attributes are removed, you are left with a pretty good kid.

Sleepy, you were good today, way to go, kid.

I continued with the other cases on my caseload, but I kept a watchful eye and ear on Sleepy's status in placement. One day I received a call from a staff member at placement and she informed me that Sleepy had made the softball team and she was pretty good! At first I didn't know what to say, I thought it was a prank. I mean, c'mon, Sleepy? Play softball? That requires hustling and the only time Sleepy ran was when the cops were chasing her or she was going to the refrigerator. When I followed up and spoke to Sleepy, she told me that she was a catcher. I just laughed. I told her how surprised I was that she was playing; she just hit me in the arm a couple of times.

Staff came up to us and expressed how good she was. I just smiled. I sat there quietly questioning staff's motives. *This is a treatment placement so is staff trying to build Sleepy's self-esteem by saying this? Is staff strengthening the relationship with her or is Sleepy really that good?* It was hard for me to believe that this lazy girl who slept in the same clothes she had worn the previous day was the catcher on a softball team. I remained in disbelief and poked fun at Sleepy with jokes like "what would the hood think?' It was a fun contact with her today.

Time at placement raced by and Sleepy had only a couple of weeks to promote from placement. I was proud of her but still disappointed. I never would have believed she would go so far as to get into trouble and have to go to placement. I didn't show my disappointment, but that's how I was feeling. I was also concerned about her returning home. Sleepy's family therapy at placement hadn't gone very well. I remember her telling me that during sessions everyone would argue and the therapist would have a hard time calming them down. So Sleepy ended up being quiet. Nine months in placement and her biggest problem still was her relationship with her mother. It had not improved that much. I was really concerned and knew Sleepy's negative spiral that got her locked up could spin out of control again with just one fight with her mom. Assisting Sleepy and her mom to reach a mutual respect and understanding was my biggest challenge. I remained optimistic and worked on a plan of action that Sleepy could follow when she returned home. At this point in our relationship, she trusted and respected me more and it was easier to get her to buy into the plan and at least try to achieve the goals outlined in the plan of action.

It was a basic plan consisting of participation in the gang program, staying off drugs, and going to school. The thought of her screwing up weighed heavily on me. Sleepy had the potential and the ability, but didn't wish to use it. How long was she going to use her mom as a crutch, choosing the wrong path and blaming her mom for her life? A part of Sleepy probably resented me for not allowing her to take the easy way out and do whatever she wanted to do. No matter what the circumstances were, I always told Sleepy that I believed in her, and I did.

One last visit I had with Sleepy before she got out of placement was very long, filled with some laughing and some crying.

It was fun to look back and recognize the steps she took and we talked about specific times. On one occasion when Sleepy was released from the hall, her mom took us to the store and bought everyone ice cream. When her mom came out with mine, she gave me a small toy fish, smaller than your hand, and it had a tape measure in it. I suppose you used the measuring tape to measure any fish you caught. Sleepy's mom knew that I loved to fish. This fish, believe it or not, would come into play in the quest to assist Sleepy in her fight for success. It was a fun afternoon that day.

Everyone kept telling me that Sleepy didn't care and I should just let her go to prison. I just couldn't believe that. I know it would have been easier for her to just be a piece of shit non-caring idiot, hooked on drugs and running with the mob and going to jail. It takes a ton of strength to do the right thing every day. It takes work to succeed. It takes a desire for more. Anyone, ANYONE, can do drugs and hang out and never work. That's the easy way out. All you have to do is breathe. That's why I say it would have been easier for sleepy to be an idiot. I made her care just enough to not throw in the towel, or at least I thought I did. I wouldn't allow her to stray that far away and I threw it in her face lots of times that it wasn't about her mother any longer. It was about her and her future. There weren't any more excuses she could use either. She couldn't use the transportation excuse for missing school because the program gave her bus passes or I would drive her. She couldn't say money was an issue because she didn't really need any. The program would also help out with a clothes voucher so that couldn't be it either. Any excuse she came up with had been placed on the table and a solution had been found. We talked about all the excuses and came to an agreement that it was just her. She had to step it up and handle her business. Sleepy would be fresh out of placement, a clean start for her.

Sleepy, what does it take to show your life can be better? What does it take to show you that your being in control of your life and succeeding will make you happier but you need to work for it? I do understand that you have spent the last five years of your life growing up in gangs, drugs, alcohol, and backyard parties. I know you were taught this lifestyle but now it is the time to turn things around before it's too late. I asked you once before and now I will ask you again. "Will you care about your life, Sleepy? Will you please care?"

CHAPTER 6

STREET LIFE

S leepy began her fresh new week by going back to school and participating in the gang program. She exhibited a positive attitude and things seemed to be in good standards at home with her mom. The gang program staff worked extremely hard to help Sleepy in some level of consistency. This alone wasn't easy because for Sleepy nothing was easy. She registered at community school and was attending Anger Management once a week. The plan of action formulated just for her required her to have daily contact with me, the last resort being a phone call. The main challenge or concern I had was the same I had before, that damn street life. The home boys and home girls who Sleepy hung out with weren't in a program and they didn't have mentors. They didn't care and wanted Sleepy back with them.

This was a tug-of-war that I had lost before and was desperately working at not losing again. I even spoke to some of her friends about drugs and gangs and tried to get them to buy into our program on their own. They respected what I was doing and preaching, but denied any help. During most of our conversations about her life I would tell her, "If you lay down with dogs, you get fleas." YOU GET FLEAS!! I pounded this thought into her head and walked away from her so-called homies and pointed out the negative comments made by her friend and his probable future. Even Sleepy could understand and recognize the negative impacts of running in that street life.

I knew she understood and I even felt as though she had started to care more, but it was going to be an uphill battle all the way. This had been the thought all along. What a struggle. Was it too much to overcome? Could she become a productive citizen and contribute positively to society? Could a rose grow in a bed of weeds? These were questions that only time could tell.

It had been almost three years that I had been working in the gang program and just short of that, working with Sleepy and her family. Over this time, relations with her family had enriched and trust was not a question any more. During most of my visits at Sleepy's house, I found myself working with nieces and nephews and other friends of the household. It was nice to be accepted and involved with their daily grind. My relationship with Sleepy continued to grow and I found myself exhibiting a fatherly approach during our interactions. One of the thoughts I had was to bring her around my own family. Over the period of working with Sleepy, my wife and kids certainly knew who she was, considering the pages beeping continually, the time I had spent with her, and all the talks my family had had over the dinner table. They knew the name and they knew the direction I wanted to see Sleepy go. I was hesitant at first because I didn't want to put an awkward pressure on Sleepy and possibly damage the rapport and respect I had with her. My theory was to show her at firsthand what a stable, drug free, working environment and family looked like. I wanted her to learn by observation. My wife decided that maybe by taking her to Disneyland with our family would be easier, and Sleepy had never been there before. What made Sleepy so special that I would involve my family with her? I honestly didn't know. I certainly hadn't done anything like this before and no other kid on my caseload was ever going to be around my family. Same question one more time... What made this girl so special?

I spoke to Sleepy about goals and school and attitude and I told her if she continued to do well, I would take her to Disneyland. At first she was shocked. Disneyland! She was excited for sure and totally agreed with maintaining status quo. The day came and in the blink of an eye we were on our way to the magic kingdom. We stopped at a hamburger stand to have lunch before we went in. Sleepy's double burger was bigger than her face and it came with a pound of fries. Sleepy was pretty happy. We entered Disneyland and my wife and I watched Sleepy and my teenaged daughter go on all the rides. It was glorious to see that smile on Sleepy's face. At one point when they were standing in line, time seemed to freeze as my thoughts captured the moment and also flashed back on Sleepy's life and her experiences. I looked at her with that smile, laughing with my daughter, just being a kid. How sad it was to remember her life of drugs, gangs, school challenges, family relationships, and those three dots tattooed on her hand. I wondered how we could secure this moment of happiness and fulfillment while living around so much negativity. I was happy for Sleepy, but I struggled with my concerns about her future. On the ride home, kids were being kids, talking about all the rides and attractions, before they nodded off. I looked in the back seat and Sleepy was tired all right. I saw the picture of them flying down Space Mountain cupped in her hand. I was happy that Sleepy had a moment that couldn't be taken away. For once, she had been a kid and had fun without drugs or alcohol. We arrived at her house to drop her off. She showed her appreciation by thanking all of us and walked into her house. I immediately recalled all the times I dropped her off with no thank you from her. I was pleased to see the respect and appreciation, and recognized some growth that I hadn't seen before.

One morning, I woke up about four a.m. Sleepy had been on my mind from the night before, I tossed and turned all night thinking about her status, the direction she was going and the conversations we had. I must have had a thousand different thoughts go through my head. What if I took her here? What if I took her there? What about Scared Straight? What if? What if?

I made coffee and sat down at the computer. I didn't really know what I was doing but I knew I had to write something. I had been fortunate to observe Sleepy at some of her best moments. I shared with her and laughed with her and realized she was a joy to be around, like the trip to Disneyland. I wanted to do something different with her, something no one else had done. I wasn't sure why, but that early morning I wrote her a poem. It is called "Struggles".

Anguish, sorrow is the struggle for tomorrow
Prayers and dreams are all we have it seems
If I were God for a day, the first thing I would do
Is spread the word from house that Jesus has plans for you.
From the time that you were born till the time that you will die,
I know you'll understand Jesus will not enjoy seeing you cry.
I'd let people know that they are not alone, Just listen to the angels sing.
Although life will be beautiful, stand strong through the struggle it will bring.
We all must face the future and we are what we make,
Just remember to keep Jesus in your heart, and your soul He'll surely take.
I'd rid the world of strife, there would be no disease
With the Lord's Prayer, I'd bring peace with the greatest of ease.
But the one thing I would make sure of, that you understand what does "struggle" mean?
When Jesus died on the cross for you, thank Him, for your soul will be clean.

So please realize that through your life, there will be some struggles you see,
Because if life was so perfect indeed, we wouldn't need anyone to set us free.

I gave this to Sleepy in hopes it would inspire her to understand that she is not the only one who sacrificed and struggled. I also gave it to her at a time when I was trying to make her understand and turn to God and use prayer for some of the problems she had and challenges she faced. It was my hope to raise her level of understanding of Jesus and what He did for us. Sleepy had fallen into a lonely place of hatred and shattered dreams. She was lost and in the dark. It was my hope to have Jesus turn on the lights. It will always be easier said than done. The struggle will always be there for all of us. The tough part is dealing with it. How can you prepare for the struggles that come in life? Good question, huh?

For me, a strong spiritual belief would first come along with values and a work ethic. If you are young, then it comes from going to school, passing classes, maybe a part-time job, no drugs, and no gangs or any other negative influences in your life. If you're older, then it's maintaining a responsible level of living. The point for all ages is just to get up and keep going forward. It's hard for a while, but it doesn't last forever unless you never try to improve your life. I believe that the more you put into your life, education, work, training, and the easier struggles will be. A person's bag of tricks is broadened and more options become available. The struggle will always find you, but will you be ready when it does?

May kids Sleepy's age don't have much going on in their lives. They party and hang out and take more time fixing their hair or downloading music than they do working on their future. Those things are OK but they need to put in some work and dedication to their future. C'mon now, you know you can't hang out and bang CD's forever. Get up, dog, and do some shit with your life. Leave the drugs alone and go to school, go to work, go anywhere, just go. The struggle will find you! If you never do anything to prepare for it, well then, may God be with you.

Street life has no end. It gets hungry and its appetite is only claiming people's lives. If you allow that lifestyle in, sooner than later it will certainly destroy you. It will rip you up and everyone around you. That's what that street lifestyle does. It doesn't love you. It wants you and thirsts to destroy you. You must know it exists, to know you need to fight it.

Getting Sleepy to realize her actions and the street life which was trying to pull her in had not been easy. She would pay heavy consequences if she didn't learn how to take one day at a time and start the fight. How could she fight "street life?" By staying clean, going to school, going to church if that was her belief, exercise, read positive things, change her friends, stop kidding herself and defending the people who weren't there for her.

A kid in placement once told me, "He is my homeboy; he will do anything for me." I said, "Great. You have been in here four months. How many times has he written to you? Zero. How many times has he mowed your mom's lawn or gone to the grocery store for her? Zero. But yet, he is your best friend. It's a mirage."

You are viewed as a good time by your so-called friends, but if it came down to it, most wouldn't remain loyal; they don't really care about you, so figure it out. They want to get high and drink and listen to music. They will do that regardless of your presence or not.

I told Sleepy when she was clean and just out of the hall, "OK, you always defend your so-called friends. You will know who really cares about you. Whoever comes up to you and asks you to get high on dope or booze, they are not your true friends. Would you agree? Sleepy stood there with a puzzled look on her face. I continued, "Look, if a friend sees you having problems with your mom and knows you've gone to the hall twice, a real friend will care about you and try to help you stay clean, go to school, and encourage you to get along with your mom. Would you agree?" Sleepy agreed. I continued, "If a so-called friend asks you to get high or commit a crime, then do they really care about you?" Sleepy said, "Probably not." So I told her, "This time, without saying a word to anyone, go about your days and write down the names of all of your so-called friends and circle the ones that don't want you to get high. Cross out all the ones who want to get high with you and do stupid stuff. Then we will see how many friends you have at the end of the week. Will you agree that the ones that end up being crossed out are not your true friends?" She replied, "No." I told her, "The street life just took another step towards you."

If Sleepy wasn't willing to drop some of the dead weight dogs that were holding on to her, then sorrow and anguish would surely follow. Street life can be beaten but you have to be serious about it. Cross out the dead weight, dude.

CHAPTER 7
SAME OL' SONG

Working intervention prevention with at risk youth is one thing, but working with gang members is a whole different ballgame. They live by different codes. Respect is a very powerful word in this lifestyle. Every member once jumped in must represent his or her hood at all time. Out of respect for the gang, members will fight, maim, or even kill someone to back their hood. Peer pressure is a major factor when these incidents arise. You see kids at school and one of them hears another kid make a negative statement about their hood. That other kid has no choice, but to attack the kid that made the remark. He may not even want to attack but knows if he or she doesn't, they will have to face other members or hierarchy of the gang. Once you allow yourself to be jumped into a gang, the expectations follow. Another important flow of gang life is "monikers" members go by. Let's say a member's moniker is "Crazy". Even if he or she didn't want to act out or fight someone, they don't really have a choice when their labeling of their gang name was "Crazy". Everyone expects and almost demands this member to be "crazy" during any issues because that's how he or she got the name. But now and even more importantly, that's how they must keep it. In most cases the member's moniker projects the type of person the member is. If it's "Crazy" then you know crazy actions will follow suit. If it's "Robbery" then you know this member is a thief, I knew one member that they called "Puppet" because when he was stoned or high on weed, he would walk really slow and dangle like a puppet.

So you ask, "What's up with Sleepy? What does this have to do with her?" I first thought she was named this because she was always sleeping in school, but Sleepy denied this. It may have been because she stayed up all night and slept all day. I don't know. Sleepy wouldn't give up the reason when I asked her. I told her the gang called her that because she was the laziest member in the gang.

What sucked was that the tug-of-war game was so strong and I was losing. Sleepy was loyal to her gang and I was running out of ideas. Like before, Sleepy would do well for a short sprint then she'd screw up one little thing and compound it by ten. Sleepy would miss one class and then decide to skip school the rest of the week because of the one missed class. She would stay clean from smoking weed for a long time and then one night she would get high and off to the races it was. She would then get high every day because her record was tarnished anyway, so why not? Sleepy always made excuses for everything and always looked for the easy way out. It was a comedy when she would get mad at me or her mom or probation concerning her screw-ups. I would just laugh really loud and get in her face and shout, "Are you crazy? Who is making the choices here? Who is calling the shots?" I would go on to tell her things like, "I didn't ditch school with you." And "I didn't smoke that joint with you." Sleepy would exhibit her natural response of walking away and being quiet. You already know the eyebrow talk and the shoulder wave was happening as well.

That is the reality of the struggles that a lot of kids including Sleepy face. It is a tug-of-war and this lifestyle of bad habits is hard to break. Add drugs to the mix and you are basically screwed. Kids' chances are very slim.

Sleepy began to sing the same old song. She continued to blame everyone else for her problems and it never got her anywhere. For the most part, I didn't blame it all on Sleepy. She did have a mother and father and it was their job to raise and educate her. They failed in my opinion. I understood it was going to take a long time to re-educate and guide her. This was a long-term case with long-term needs. The thing that was so upsetting was she was getting older and had experienced the hall and placement enough times, but still couldn't seem to get on track. How hard was it to go to school and stay off drugs? I did blame Sleepy for not caring enough about her future, but I recognized her mom and dad's efforts or lack of, as poor as they were. Week after week, I would go from being positive and proud to frustrate and pissed off. Sleepy would show signs of success and then screw up ten-fold in the same week. This drove me up a freaken wall. She would go to school, have two or three good days, test negative for probation, and attend components. Then, in the next three days, she would ditch class, smoke out with her homies, and then lie to me when I confronted her. She didn't seem to care when I yelled at her. Sleepy was headed for the hall once again. Probation quickly grew tired of her weekly roller coaster ride and locked her up again. I was happy with that because it gave me time to re-think the whole situation and I knew she was safe in there. "Man, just use some of that potential!" were most of my prayers. Sleepy was always in my prayers.

I kept busy working on the next plan of action while the little princess was in custody. I concentrated on the circle of people that Sleepy would go back into. I met with school officials and campus security. I met with Probation and component counselors. I even spoke to her brother and some homies in her gang. The goal was to have everyone on the same page working together towards the same goal. In this case, it was called "keep Sleepy out of jail".

In comparison to today, this would be called a collaborated effort and/or MDT- multi disciplinary team and/or the newly used "Wraparound" approach. This Wraparound approach is currently being used everywhere now. It basically recognizes one's strength and wraps a team of people around that one individual. I did the same thing for Sleepy, but I called it "Mikearound." There were several teachers who gave Sleepy a zero out of ten to succeed. I quickly worked with school staff to have Sleepy reassigned to different teachers.

You see the problem here though. Even if the kid wanted to change, you'll always have that one teacher who won't give them a chance. Kids like Sleepy who need encouragement, find more criticism from ones who should be their biggest supporter- their teacher. You would think a highly educated person would realize where the fault lies with these kids and the kids can't change with help and support. I must have asked four or five teachers why they got into teaching.

I was glad I had contacted all these people. It was interesting to hear their comments on their perceptions of Sleepy and her world. They didn't know her like I did. They only knew a careless gang member/thug. They had never heard any of Sleepy's dreams or her personal perception of life. I also even sent a plan of action to the judge as well. I wanted everyone in on it. The problem I saw was I had shown the entire plan I had with this girl and I knew the judge wouldn't be lenient in dealing with her, knowing what was being offered to her. If Sleepy got out and didn't take advantage of the opportunities offered to her, including job development, then she needed to be locked up. "Good luck when you get out, you hairy gangster".

By the way, Sleepy had never commented on her list of so-called friends that she was supposed to circle or cross out. I was betting she didn't have any friends left on the list after two days.

Sleepy got out and was rushed into several different components. She was assisted with school and showed only minimal progress, as usual. Her attitude was OK and her relationship with her mom wasn't good or bad, just whatever. She continued to go out at night which affected her mornings, because of her late hours, and if she showed up at school, she was always late. I did talk to her, but decided to take a back seat this time around. I allowed her to decide how she wanted to handle her terms and conditions of probation. Her mom and the school would call me, and I told them I would talk to her. I didn't yell or preach to her. I just explained to her the steps she had taken and her history and the direction she was headed. I also told her I liked it when she was locked up because I always knew where to find her. I told her good luck and she knew where to find me if she needed help. She did well for about a week. I knew a Doberman named Roxiedog that worked harder at doing the right thing.

CHAPTER 8

GROUP HOME

Yea, she blew it again and here we were in court, again. Even the judge didn't know what to do with her. The next step was to remove her from her home. The judge ordered a six month group home setting in Moreno Valley. It was a house setting in a regular neighborhood. The neighborhood was actually very nice with well-maintained landscapes. Sleepy had her own room despite five other girls that also lived in the house.

After two weeks of Sleepy being there, I called and introduced myself to one of the owners. We spoke for a while; discussing Sleepy's past and then discussed her current status and attitude. The owner was new at this because the home had only been in operation for about a year. I explained that Sleepy needed to be pressured and there could be no wiggle room. Rules were rules and she needed to follow them. Driving away I had several thoughts about Sleepy, her family, the group home, and probation. I was staying positive and I reminded myself that she had a safe place to stay, three meals a day and would be watched 24/7. I just couldn't believe the talk I had with Sleepy before I left. She was mad and irritated at me. We had disagreed about her status and how her actions had led her to the Group Home. Sleepy even yelled at me,

"No one told you to come here." I just laughed at her, which upset her even more. I told her to shut her mouth and not talk unless she had something positive to say.

Kids that are in crisis lash out and when they do, it leaves the people who are trying to help them just shaking their heads, asking themselves, "What the heck is going on?" I had been yelled at plenty of times by that girl. Why? Because I was the constant bearer of responsibility and accountability, the two words Sleepy couldn't stand. Whenever you hold any irresponsible person accountable for their actions, it causes friction.

I spoke to Sleepy the following week. As usual we talked about our argument. Points were made, and then we changed the subject. I had been in contact with the owner of the group home to check on Sleepy's status. I had also spoken to the Probation officer assigned to the home. The officer was experienced, patient, and she seemed to care more than the others. We got along and I enjoyed seeing her and speaking to her. I believed this home would be a good change for Sleepy. It wasn't Placement and it wasn't Juvenile Hall. The Group Home gave the kids more room to move, to be themselves, but also applied discipline and structure in the girls' lives. These were two things that Sleepy needed. It was a house setting, which I really liked. It was a four bedroom, two baths with a good sized back yard. It was in a nice neighborhood and I felt Sleepy would do well there. There were five other girls there that Sleepy had to live with but it wasn't like she was locked up and confined to a cell. The girls were allowed to go places, but they had to go together. After a few weeks, Sleepy was sporting new clothes and she had her nails done. She looked OK and seemed to get along with most of the other girls. The lady who ran the house was very nice and seemed to know what she was doing. She had all the girls on a short leash seemed to have a good relationship with them. I was happy that Sleepy liked them and I felt it would help her get through the next six months.

I continued to work with the other clients on my caseload. I monitored Sleepys weekly status with the staff at the Group Home. I also continued to have home contacts at Sleepy's house, talking to her sister, nieces and nephews. I felt it was extremely important to continue to build relationships within Sleepy's family. I would talk to Sleepy's sister about jobs and school, and how she could have better things if she landed a better job, in her case, any job. I spoke to Sleepy's niece Selena about the dangers of drugs and gang life and about the steps in Sleepy's life and the impact of each of her actions. For the most part, I believed they knew I cared.

I always left their house with feelings of confusion, hopelessness, and despair. The house was dirty and trashy, no one was employed, the yard was dirt, and it reminded me of a third world country; poverty stricken, deplorable conditions, and no one striving for anything. I'm sorry if you think I shouldn't put down the way some people live. Well, I believe no one should live like pigs, do drugs, and raise children in that atmosphere. How many times had Sleepy's sister re-assigned her kids in school? How many times had the kids missed school because of their mother's issues? Several times a week, they would have a kick back (party) at the house. I guess they felt they deserved it. Nevertheless, this was Sleepy's family. It was where she had been raised and they were a big part of her life and a major cause of her problems. As I said before, my dad always said, "If you lay down with dogs – you get fleas." What if the dogs are your family, and then what do you do?

You can have generational meaning for just about anything. You know things you pass down from one generation to the next. In Sleepy's case, the actions, the actions that were passed from Sleepy and her sisters did not need to be passed down the chute to the younger ones. It just didn't need to happen.

I could already see the impact on Sleepy's nieces and nephews. The kids were learning bad habits and it wasn't good. Kids learn from observing. Let's see, we drink all the time, we don't work, and we wait for the government check. We have to move every four months or so because we don't use the money that is given to us to pay the rent, so we get evicted. We don't clean the house. We curse all the time and oh yea, we hate the cops. The kids pick this all up and believe it is the way it is and should be.

That's why there are group homes and out-of-home placements for these kids. Their home life isn't giving them what they need. I shared these facts with Sleepy and others in her family. They didn't listen. Sleepy was in a Group Home for this reason. It was only for six months and she could do that standing on her head. I just wondered what in the heck we were going to do when she got out. Nothing was changing at home. "You are tiring me out, hairy gangster."

Group Home life for the most part was good for Sleepy. She was counting her days, don't get me wrong. But she seemed OK living there. Sleepy was doing OK in school too. She was testing negative for drugs and her PO was pleased with her status. I was pleased to hear the positive comments and urged her to be consistent. I would visit when I could but managed phone calls as a last resort.

The time was racing by and I knew he six months would be up. I attempted to plan the steps she would need to take when she completed the Group Home. What I didn't know was that Sleepy had a plan too.

I spent the next three months making visits to the home and speaking with her on the phone. I actually had several contacts with Sleepy's niece Selena. I helped her with her times tables and other school work. Like I said before, Selena was a nice kid who showed compassion and appreciation. I grew close to her as the visits continued.

CHAPTER 9

SAME OLD SONG –AGAIN !

Time had gone by quickly. Days turned to weeks and weeks turned to months and Sleepy was about to leave the Group Home. She was something else. She needed more help than anyone, but she managed to persuade Probation and the owner of the group Home that she wanted to go back to school and start on time for a change, which meant she would have to leave her house earlier. I didn't understand it but they let her do it. She had completed four months in the Group Home and I went with her mom to pick her up. Boy, what a surprise we got when we first saw her that day. They gave her a small promotion ceremony, and Sleepy- hairy gangster- was wearing a dress. You heard me; she was sporting a dress and heels. She looked pretty, but at the same time it didn't look like her. The Home had taken her to a salon to have her hair and nails done, and she was all duddied up. I laughed a little and made fun of her. I said things like, "Hey, Sleepy, what about the hood, eh? They see you like this; they'll kick your ass! I guess you ain't down, eh?" Sleepy just laughed as we left the compound.

I drove to her house and Sleepy changed out of her Elvira outfit and we sat around and talked for a couple of hours. We discussed everything she had gone through up to that point. We talked about different strategies and we developed a plan of action (again!) that we believed would work and then we went to get something to eat. Sleepy had the same thing as always, cheeseburger, fries, and a Sprite. We ate, talked, and when we finished we decided to cruise the neighborhood. We observed the tagging of gang names and we talked about the gangs and drug use. Sleepy spotted one of her friends walking. I told Sleepy she was a cross off on the list friend and Sleepy called her a circle friend and told me to shut up. We stopped to say hello. I knew this girl from being around Sleepy's family so much. The girl was happy to see Sleepy and told her about a kick back they were going to have later that night. We drove away and Sleepy was quiet. I reminded Sleepy of her friends comment and how that's all these people want to do. Sleepy didn't even respond. I kept driving down the streets and I reflected on everything that had happened in the past and I felt sick. Maybe it was her attitude, not that it had been horrible, I just thought she should have made some strong, positive comments to that girl, such as her school or work. Instead the conversation had been about the neighborhood, whom had gotten her locked up while she was in the Group Home, and who was going to be at the party. Am I wrong or is that a bunch of crap? After all the time I spent on her, after all the lockdowns and placement, all the family problems and dysfunctional lifestyle, she still chose that thought process.

We continued to drive around, and I felt really confused. I felt that I had wasted my time and that all the comments my peers and my boss had made about Sleepy were true. Was this whole "counseling father" thing become about me and my ego, an "I must succeed" kind of thing, I am the best and therefore the worst (Sleepy) cannot fail, she will make it and live free and sober and peaceful. I just kept driving and Sleepy turned the radio on.

I then started asking myself questions. How could I spend so much time with this kid and have the worst results of any of the kids I worked with? Had she manipulated me? No way, not this hard-core, old school Italian. I had always been hard on her. We had more shouting matches than I could count. I always expected more of her. I pushed myself to do more when it came to her. You know, the rose in a bed of weeds thing. Never give up, no matter what. For the first time since I met this yawning girl, I started to second guess myself. I really needed to step back and analyze this situation and be true to myself.

I casually looked over at Sleepy, she was quietly singing along with the song on the radio. She seemed at peace, was enjoying herself and I had just struggled and fought a war within myself. I searched for answers and I suddenly grew tired. I drove up to Sleepy's house to drop her off. I told her I would be out of town for a while, up north fishing and she wouldn't be able to get ahold of me. Sleepy asked about my cell phone and I told her I wasn't taking it with me. She just looked at me with a quizzical frown and then walked away. I didn't say anything else and I drove away. The truth of the matter was I didn't want to be bothered. I didn't want to deal with her as I was refueling my own mind, my own spirit, and my own needs. I needed time to think and I knew catching some fish and camping by the river with my partner was just what I needed. It would give me a chance to review the whole situation with my buddy Jimmy, and I would have an easier time deciding which direction I was going to take.

Jimmy and I caught a bunch of fish and set off back to the campsite for dinner. I made some trout and rice, as I am usually the cook. Jimmy provided the beverages from the ice chest when I was thirsty. We ate dinner and stretched out in the lounge chairs by the riverbank. We were in the middle of nowhere and we seemed to be the only ones around for miles. The river was beautiful and peaceful, running from north to south. The stars were out and their divine glow showered across the sky. It was pure serenity as I saw it, and Jimmy and I talked about how beautiful it was.

Jim then asked how Sleepy was doing and then chuckled as if to say, "Should I even ask?" I took a slug of my beer and threw another log on the campfire. I told him about the Group Home and that Sleepy had gotten out early. Jim knew all about Sleepy, had met her, talked to her, and knew her whole story. I filled him in on all the details and that I was concerned about her true desires to do the right thing and that I thought she really didn't care. Jimmy responded by saying, "You have been trying to show her the way the other side of life can be, so now it's up to her." I agreed, but it didn't change the fact that my feelings of her not caring enough were real and I was fighting with myself about giving up on her. I really didn't want to. I really cared about Sleepy and her family, but I felt I was beating my head against a brick wall for no reason at all.

The four days at the river passed too quickly. We had thoroughly enjoyed ourselves, but it was time to head for home. I was hungry to get back to work, not so much for Sleepy, but I had other kids and families I dealt with, and to tell you the truth, I missed them. I did agree with Jimmy that I needed to give more time to the other kids on my caseload and not spend all my time on the "Sleepy" project. He reminded me that Sleepy did need me even though she may not show it. I reluctantly agreed.

I made it back to work the following week and was notified by Probation that Sleepy wasn't doing too good. She had missed her appointments, hadn't attended school, and had made no contact with the Probation Department. It didn't take Sleepy too long to screw things up. Right out of the gate, just like a quarter horses, she had stumbled, and nothing that followed was positive. I wanted to shoot her all right. She had started hanging out with the mob, wasn't attending school, and word on the street was she was doing speed. I couldn't believe it; I took it personal. She had taken off and no one knew where she was. I contacted her brother, Midnight, and he was even having trouble finding her. I heard he even beat up five of the other members who were trying to protect her, because they lied to him about her whereabouts. Says went by and I became angrier and angrier.

I had other cases I worked with that would tell me little things here and there like, "Sleepy's really tearing it up out there this time." And "she's smoking it and selling it." They also said, "Sleepy kicked another homies' ass last night." All I could do was just smile and say, "What a waste." Inside I was screwed up, I wanted to go away and hide. This time she had really done it. She wouldn't call, Midnight couldn't find her, and the members of her gang were helping her. I had absolutely no plan, and for the first time I was truly afraid for her safety.

I still had the little fish measuring tape that Sleepy's mom had given me. I pulled it out, turned it over and wrote on the back of it, "I still believe in you." I gave it to one of her homeboys who I knew would find her. I told him to give it to her and tell her that even though she screws up she didn't need to throw in the towel and also tell her that I was praying for her.

Weeks went by and word came down from the streets that she was in Oxnard and was jumped by another gang and was beat up pretty bad. Through all of this, I continued to work with other clients on my caseload, but my heart just wasn't in it. I was just going through the motions. Not to mention my boss and everyone else telling me how right they were and Sleepy was a piece of shit. Let's not forget the PO who got her out of the Group Home. She was upset because she, too, had tried to help Sleepy. For the first time, I had no defense for all the attacks and comments about Sleepy.

Sleepy's mom would call me from time to time, and mostly apologize for her daughter. She would also thank me for trying to help. I felt beaten. I felt I had lost the tug-of-war and that damned street life had claimed another victim. There was no stopping it.

It was at times like this that I asked God, "Why, why put me into this girl's life for this?" I had difficulty understanding why, out of all of my caseload, I would make Sleepy the most important one. I prayed for a solution, but I guess I was blinded to the answer.

I couldn't believe how fast things had changed. Sleepy was doing really well a few weeks back. She was going to school. She was clean and attending her counseling and anger management classes. She had a positive attitude and appeared happy. I had that fleeting moment of pride that the Group Home experience had been good for her. But in the blink of an eye, she had a warrant out for her arrest and was somewhere all beat up. This had turned into a real nightmare. I continued to tell myself and my co-workers that when someone deserves your love the least, it is the time they need it the most. It made sense, but man, was it hard to follow.

A month went by and the phone rang. It was Sleepy. She was quiet and sounded confused. Even though she had called me, she didn't have much to say. For the first time I didn't have much to say either. I told her this wasn't what I had taught her and I was disappointed. I also told her she should turn herself in. Sleepy said she was tired and she would turn herself in, but I didn't believe her. She was out of control. She sounded like another person and I could tell she was under the influence.

The following week her mom called me and said that Sleepy was at the house, showering and wanted to let me know that. I advised her mother to call Probation right away and have them lock Sleepy up for her own protection. Her mom disagreed with me and was upset, but reluctantly made the call. Probation showed up and Sleepy jumped out the back window and hid under a car. She was in the same parking lot as the officers. All the officers had to do was bend down and look under the van that was parked in front of the house and they would have seen her. They looked around for a short time and then they left without finding Sleepy. She was angry with her mom for calling them. Her mom stood her ground and told Sleepy to turn herself in. Her mother told me they argued for a while, and then Sleepy vanished again.

Several weeks passed and I continued to hear the word from the street concerning Sleepy. You know it was never good. Finally, Sleepy was known to hang out in a certain hotel and Probation was sent there. Luckily, they arrested her this time and took her to Juvenile Hall. I was happy because I knew at least she would be safe. I must admit my feelings for her at this point were bleak. I tried to build up some kind of faith, but it just wasn't there.

Her roll was finally stopped. Now my prayers were, "Please God, don't let there be any new offenses or crimes while she was out there." I allowed two weeks to go by before I contacted her in Juvi. I wanted her brain to be sober and her thoughts to be clear. I asked her why she did the things she did. She first stated that she didn't know and then replied, "I missed one day of school and got high on weed and I felt like I blew it, so I said screw it."

Well for those of you who may get a chance to read this one day, I say it's OK to screw up once in a while. It's not easy to change a life, or a generation, but you must believe that if Monday is a bad day, maybe Tuesday will be better. Don't throw away the whole basket of apples because only one of them is bad. Jus cut out the bad spot and move forward. No one expects you to be perfect, but people will expect an effort. On the other hand, it's really easy to skip classes, get high, and hang out with the mob. It takes a powerful person and a powerful desire to want more out of life. I know how difficult it is to do the right thing. That's why there are so many losers out there, because it is so easy to be one.

Although Sleepy is a very special and unique case, I've heard this same response from a thousand other kids. When these kids start to do well, their so-called friends get on them and pressure them. They end up bringing them down. They make them feel that they are betraying the gang, the street, and even their own families. These "friends" are dogs that have fleas and they need their own outreach worker and program.

Remember the lines and circles? When a family does not provide discipline and structure at a young age and the problems mount as the child reaches adolescence, there will only be danger ahead. The gang, or kids that follow in the same upbringing, will find each other. The drugs and alcohol and stupid thinking will take over, and then the kids' reputations are built. That's the rep the kids have to live up to, even if they find themselves wanting to change. The power of who they are now is sometimes too much to overcome.

This might happen to Sleepy. She had all the makings of a gang leader. She also still had the ability and intelligence to succeed and live a comfortable life. The tug-of-war continued, destination unknown.

CHAPTER 10

PLACEMENT

I let a full month go by before I went to see Sleepy in the Hall. She looked pathetic, embarrassed, stupid and tired. I told her how she made all of us feel and if she didn't care about her life and wanted to trash it, to go ahead, go for it. I told her they build prisons for people like that and she would fit right in. I stood up and said I was hoping some sense had been knocked into her by the Oxnard gang. She looked up at me, surprised that I knew. She asked me how I had found out. I just told her that when a person really cares about someone, it's easy to find answers.

Sleepy was not happy. She did not want to be in the Hall and didn't like the fact that the judge had told her she was going to Placement. Sleepy didn't want any part of Placement and sat there with a bewildered look. She was totally overwhelmed. She was beat up from the neighborhood, used up by drugs, tired from the dysfunction of her family, and frustrated with the justice department. It was all on her front step; all right in her face. I must admit, it felt good to see her finally hurt some. Even as I sat there looking at her, being mad at her, and just wanting to slap her, I found a speck of compassion and tried to offer some unconditional love through some kind words. It was tough to do, but I remembered the first time I met Sleepy and her family. I knew the problems the family had and it was not surprising that Sleepy was going down the path she was on. I still felt she should be doing better but she hadn't made any effort. I told her she was in my prayers and I left.

The next day Sleepy got word from her PO. She was told she would be going to a Placement Home in Hemet. It was a ranch setting that offered clients working with animals. I thought this would be good for her, it sounded great. Sleepy's mother called me later that afternoon. She said she had spoken to Sleepy and she didn't really want to go to the ranch and asked if there was anything I could do to prevent it. I just laughed and told Sleepy's mom, "Oh well."

Sleepy was moved to the Hall in a matter of days. I concentrated on my caseload, but I kept thinking of Sleepy, and it made me smile to picture her milking a cow or feeding the pigs.

A couple of days passed and I made arrangements to see Sleepy at her new placement. My boss and I were set to visit at the end of the following week. This would give her some time to adapt to the place and get settled in.

I finished my day at work and started the drive home. I went to see Sleepy's family and my main concern was Selena, Sleepy's niece. I wasn't sure which direction she was headed. She had been brought up the same way and that was a problem.

I drove home, ate a nice dinner with my family, discussed daily activities with my kids, kissed my wife goodnight, and went to bed. About 7:30pm the phone rang and it was; you guessed it, Sleepy. She was calling form a pay phone. She had run away from Placement and was in downtown Hemet at a fast food restaurant. My wife, who had answered the phone, told Sleepy that I wasn't home and asked her what she wanted. Sleepy said she would call back later. My wife told me about the call and I was furious. Sleepy called back about 10:30. I yelled at her and she asked me to get in touch with her mom. I ended up calling her mom and told her the situation and that Sleepy needed to be picked up. Her mom said their car wasn't working, and asked if I could pick her up and we would both go to pick up Sleepy. I was hesitant but finally agreed. We arrived in Hemet and couldn't find Sleepy. After driving around for an hour or so, Sleepy came walking out of the side of a building and got into the car. Her mom and I talked to her and told her she needed to go back to the Placement Home. Sleepy was adamant about not going back, so I just drove them to their house. Sleepy swore she would turn herself in on Monday, but I didn't trust or believe her, and I told her this. Her mom accepted what Sleepy said so I left it up to them. I told them the damned street life was taking another bite and she was allowing it. I dropped them off, and Sleepy came around to my side of the car and hugged me and thanked me and said she could always count on me.

I drove away with an array of thoughts and feelings. I was angry at myself for helping her, but at the same time I had to look at this as some kind of victory, meaning the trust she had in me.

The two main things I set out to do with not only Sleepy, but the other kids on my caseload, were to gain their trust and gain their respect. It wasn't an easy task, but it was what I had to do if I was ever going to help them. Sleepy had learned that she could count on me more than any of her family. She knew I would back up my words with actions. She didn't feel she could count on her mom and that was a big part of the problem. I didn't repeat the rules and regulation talk, Sleepy had already heard it. I kept trying to find a positive in this virtually negative situation.

Halloween was three days away, on a Tuesday, so I wanted to see Sleepy turn herself in on Monday. There was no way she was going to do that. She could barely turn herself in on a normal day, so she definitely wasn't going to on the day before "spook night." This was the one night she could totally be herself.

My phone rang and it was her. She again thanked me for picking her up, but explained that she would turn herself in on Wednesday because she had forgotten about Halloween. (I called that one, huh) I just started laughing and said, "Yea, great, have a wonderful night." She just said that actions speak louder than words. I had my doubts, to say the least.

Wednesday morning came, I didn't hear from anyone until that afternoon. Sleepy's mom called me to tell me she had dropped Sleepy off at Probation and they took her to Juvenile Hall. No way, Jose. I couldn't believe it. She really did turn herself in. I would have bet a thousand dollars against that one. It showed me that even though she was out of control and ran from Placement, and so on and so on; she could muster up some strength to face her consequences.

I guess God really doesn't put anything in front of you that He doesn't believe you can overcome. Sleepy was a prime example of that.

I was hoping Sleepy was thinking about all that crap she had been through. I was wishing she would just go to school, stay off drugs, and go to church. For years I had been preaching to her about this. Like most kids in trouble, she had skills and potential. It was hard to get her to care about herself.

Let's look at this; if you fell in a hole filled with mud and crap, the first thing you would do when you crawled out would be to take a shower and change clothes. Now, look at life's problems and challenges the same way. Removing all this messiness could change your outlook on life. What if you set goals and involved someone who really cared about you in your life? A mentor could be a strong force, but you must open your heart and be honest with yourself. You want to know what the biggest obstacle is. You have changed your thoughts and appearance and your direction in life but no one else did. Your so-called friends, and even your family, are the ones who will bring you down. Thank you for nodding and agreeing.

The world's perception of you will not change until you prove to everyone that you have changed. Teachers will still think of you in the same way, grocery store clerks will still keep an eye on you when you enter the store. You have to prove that you are on the straight and narrow, and it is a very difficult thing to change your image. It can be achieved but you need to stay busy with your life; school, work, church, whatever it is that is positive to keep you moving forward to a goal. You can never stop fighting the dangerous lifestyle. Go ahead and try the other side. See what it has to offer, maybe beauty and peace.

CHAPTER 11
DÉJÀ VU

A couple of weeks went by and I went to the Hall to have a contact with Sleepy. My hope was she would be displaying a better attitude by now. Visits to the hall usually slowed her down a bit and her attitude improved. Sleepy walked out all chained up and she looked a little older. She appeared worn down and didn't exhibit the "I'm hard and no one messes with me" look her body movements usually suggested. She waddled her way to the bench and even yawned as she approached. Well, that part was the same.

I asked her before she sat down if I should prepare myself for visits with her in County Jail. She responded with a quiet "no". She was withdrawn as if she hadn't had much sleep. I told her if she didn't change her lifestyle and habits, County Jail was a reality. It was time to wake up. I told her how much I cared for her and I recognized the strengths she had, but she frustrated me with her irresponsible actions. I explained how hard it was to maintain the caring attitude when the person you were trying to help didn't seem to care back.

Sleepy commented that she did care, she just got caught up. It was quiet for a moment as others in the Hall walked close by. There were about fifteen girls, ages twelve to eighteen. They had to walk with their hands behind their backs and follow structure. I heard a guard yells out, "Keep your heads forward, please."

I looked at Sleepy and said, "You are looking at yourself."

She just smiled, and then she said something that made me smile. "I am the one that has fleas because I keep lying down with dogs."

I laughed and told her she may not follow what I say but at least she was listening. We spoke for a short time and then I told her I needed to leave. I told her to go ahead and walk away first. Sleepy looked at me with a puzzled expression. I said I wanted her to go first so that when I told the other girls on my caseload about her; I wanted to get the chains down so I could repeat it to them accurately. I told her every negative situation has a positive roll to it.

I told Sleepy, "Look at your situation. You have potential and you are smart, but you would rather be in chains. Well, I have a twelve year old that I am working with who thinks she wants to be the next Sleepy. I will share all your stories and custody time with her in hopes it will change the direction she is going. I am taking your negative situation and making it a positive one for her."

Sleepy told me I was strange. We both laughed and she waddled away. She had gone about fifteen feet when I yelled at her to come back and walk for me again. Sleepy just shook her head and continued walking. I left thinking to myself, "Man I love this girl, but what a pain in the ass."

Sleepy's court date arrived and I attended. I sat in the back way of the courtroom. The judge knew Sleepy well and gave her an ultimatum and explained the concerns the court had. He then ordered Sleepy to Placement once again. This was no surprise since Sleepy had violated every term on her probation letter. The judge also helped her out by sending her to the same Placement she had already graduated from. Sleepy turned to me in the back row and she smiled. I knew Sleepy had liked this place and had gotten along with most of the staff. It was another nine month program and she would be transported there the next day.

I had mixed emotions. I knew how intelligent she was and when she tried she could pass school but yet, here we were in court going to Placement again. I saw the image of her family, the lawlessness, the drug use, the zero guidance, and I thought "It could be worse". I felt guilt and remorse that if I had only gotten to her at an earlier age, would she still be in this situation? If her dad had cared and wasn't a heroin addict, where would she be now? My sympathetic heart and my compassion for her were overwhelming.

I smiled back at Sleepy as if to say, "Yea, you'll be OK." I left the courtroom and that same feeling of being beaten overpowered me. I sensed that street life laughing and gloating, my only defense being a positive attitude and trusting in God. I still felt Sleepy was the one who needed to start caring more.

A couple of weeks went by and I gave Sleepy time to make the transition into the Placement. I finished the week off and then I stopped by to see her. It had been a while since we had spoken and I was anxious to see her. I had heard she had made the Placement softball team and I wanted her to tell me about it.

I entered the Placement and talked to the main staff who knew me. I asked about Sleepy and if it was a good time for a visit. The staff explained to me that I was not allowed to see her because I had changed jobs. I asked to speak to the supervisor, who reiterated what the staff had told me. I explained my history of working with Sleepy, the father figure, mentor, etc. I was willing to have staff supervised visits. I tried everything I could think of. They simply would not let me see her. I was pretty pissed off. They just said those were the rules and I did understand rules. However, I thought our situation was unique and because Sleepy had been there before and they knew me, we had a relationship.

Then it hit me like a ton of bricks. The first time Sleepy had been in Placement, they had denied me contact as well. However, due to the fact that the gang program was a court ordered pro-gram, contact was to be honored and they were forced to let me see her. I had had to get the paperwork from the judge and meet with the director to allow visitation. Placement didn't like the fact that they had been court ordered and they resented that they had to let me see Sleepy. Now it was a different situation because of my job change. As I continued to work with kids on my caseload and develop action plans, I also developed one for myself. I was hired by the San Bernardino Probation Department to be a correctional officer in Juvenile Hall.

I looked at the staff standing there with the supervisor and I made one last comment. I told them that I understood their rules but they did have the power to allow me visits because they knew me from before. (I don't know how they knew I had changed jobs.) I explained the amount of time I had worked with Sleepy, and how sad it was that so many of these kids needed mentors and father figures and guidance, etc., etc. They just shook their heads no.

I muttered some profanities and walked off. I was angry for Placement denying me, so I did what any other person in my po-sition would do. I went around them. I arranged for a friend in probation in their city to pick up Sleepy and bring her to his office (which was next door to Placement). The probation officer picked Sleepy up the following Friday and brought her to his office. I had my visit with Sleepy, and many more visits in the same manner the entire time she was in Placement, and no one found out! I did what I had to do, given I had no other options. I felt it was another rough time in her life and she still needed the support of the fa-ther figure I represented. The friend who helped me understood the relationship I had with Sleepy and he knew why contacts were so important. In fact, he stayed with us to visit each time, enjoying the lunch I brought, (everyone has their price). Sometimes rules are made to be broken.

Sleepy's placement was for nine months just like before. She had already completed it once and she knew she could do it again. I used my PO friend once a month to have contact with Sleepy for four months, then she earned passes and I didn't have to use my friend as much.

Sleepy did have more problems in Placement this time around with staff and other girls locked up there. I'm sure she used the "I've been here before and I know the staff, so shut up and sit down" attitude. I know I said she earned passes, but the staff probably gave them to her just to get rid of her. These breaks were for the staff, disguised as "Good job, Sleepy". I knew of other Placements where kids would earn passes home and the staff would chant, "Don't come back, don't come back, and don't come back." They probably chanted something similar in Sleepy's case. I told Sleepy she had to deal with all the issues and I threw in the "You're an idiot" part because she was the one who got herself into the mess.

"Oh, nobody understands," she would whine. "Bull-ony", I would retort. "Family issues- yes, but did you make things worse by doing drugs and being involved in gangs, and committing crimes? Could you be in a regular school passing your classes? Yes. Could you listen and follow rules? No. Is your dad on heroin; is your mom weak and helpless to help you because of her own issues? Yes. You know all this. You are SMART and you just said, 'Screw it! I'm just going to be a piece of shit' Well that is crappolla! Just because your family sucks doesn't mean you have to be like them. You can't get them to care about you or give you attention just by getting into more trouble."

I told her she was headed for the Youth Authority if she didn't change her ways and to take her frustrations out on the softball field and leave them there. Sleepy had made the team once again, playing catcher and third base. It was hard to believe this lazy gangster was moving fast anywhere. The only time I saw her run was to the refrigerator at home or when we went for fast food and she ran from the car to the front doors of the building.

Sleepy was also involved in the marching band. Since Placement was similar to boot camp, they did marching like ROTC. About a month later, Sleepy was going to march in a parade in Cherry Valley. I decided to take my wife and kids to check it out. We saw Sleepy marching with a big smile on her face. It was good to see her happy, just being a normal kid for the day. It was almost surreal. At the end of the parade, Sleepy's group was in a circle getting ready to leave. I slowly approached her to say hello. The staff saw me and stepped in front of her and directed me away from her. I asked if my wife and I could talk to her if staff stayed with us. They just responded no. They didn't say it like "No sir, we need the kids to be structured and we are counting them all the time but we appreciate your supporting her so just say hi and then please leave." It was a flat out NO, and they were still staring back at me. My wife even commented, "Wow, you guys are too much."

At that point I looked at Sleepy and told her I was proud of her, she looked great, and asked her if she was doing OK. Staff attempted to intervene but I just kept talking to her regardless of their efforts. I instructed Sleepy not to talk to me so she wouldn't get into trouble. Staff called their supervisor over and as the supervisor tried to talk to me, my wife engaged her in conversation so I could still talk to Sleepy. I just kept talking as they were loading the girls into the vans. I smiled at the staff and told them to have a nice day. It was great to see her and fun as hell to work the staff into a frenzy. Not once did staff tell Sleepy to turn around and get into the van. They focused on me, trying to control me. C'mon staff, you can't control anyone but those kids you have in custody. Geeze Louise. Give me a break. It didn't dampen our spirits at all. My whole family stood there and waved goodbye as Sleepy's van drove away. We even beeped at them on the freeway because we took the same route home. It was hilarious. We waved bye to the staff too. They sent us dirty looks. They probably took their frustrations out on Sleepy, but I told her they would. I told her to stay quiet during their later questioning of the incident, because she for once didn't do anything wrong. (I can't imagine Sleepy keeping quiet.) I guess I can be a stinker at times, but my intentions are never malicious and my focus is always on the betterment of the kid.

Days turned into months, and before I knew it Sleepy was about to complete her time in Placement. Although she was going to be free again, she was afraid. She really didn't want to mess up again and since nothing had changed at her house and the relationship with her mom was the same, it scared her. At this point in Sleepy's life, she was well aware of the problems associated with lying down with dogs. The majority of her teenage years had been spent in lockup and having problems with law enforcement. I spoke with Sleepy one more time before her release. I told her to focus on the things she needed to do and what she could gain by making good decisions and the impact that would have on her life. It was a good talk and brought tears of hope to our eyes. Here we were, back to the same word I had been driving into for years, CARE. That was the hardest thing for her to do.

Sleepy had done well and I was proud of her. She looked good – healthy and refreshed. I told her to relax with her family and I would catch up with her the following week. What was my plan of action? I had no idea.

The girl had been through the woodworks of therapy and counseling. She had been talked to a million times. It was funny though, I still didn't know if Sleepy cared about her life and her future. It all boiled down to her feelings and actions and desires. I did feel optimistic about her chances. I felt she had grown a little and maybe it was time for change. I thought that was what she wanted but how much of an effort was she able to put forth? Only time would tell. I hoped she would choose wisely, or her future could be more nightmares.

I would make believe and fast forward her life and always imagine the worst case scenario. Then I would look at her and tell her about a different life image of her succeeding and ask her which one she wanted. She would always pick the second. Maybe she was only telling me what she knew I wanted to hear. I had used this scenario talk on hundreds of kids and they would all pick the better life, but then most of them would go back and do the same stupid things they had done before, things that got them in trouble. I never could understand why these kids would do this. I knew every one of them had their own story and issues, but if they knew what the cause of their troubles were; why not change things and take power over their own lives? And if they couldn't, then ask for professional help.

I have a friend whose family is very dysfunctional, into drugs, crime, and the general drama. Yet this person gets up every day, goes to work, and has never been in trouble. He has made the right decisions and has power over his life. That has been his decision. It depends on the individual and his or her desires, period. What do you want out of life? If you have made bad decisions and are involved in gangs, drugs, crime, and you want out, wean yourself away from this. Use any excuse you can, school, job, family, anything, keep yourself busy taking care of the most important person, yourself! Where there is a will, there is a way.

CHAPTER 12

CHANGE OF RESIDENCE

Sleepy had finished Placement on schedule. She completed nine months of boot camp, intense counseling, family therapy, individual therapy, drug counseling and another load of components. I recognized her achievements and gave her some kudos. It was a good thing that she had completed the program. You must remember that some of the clients in that Placement failed and were sent back to the Hall or the California Youth Authority. I prayed that this was it and Sleepy was going to turn her life around. The little princess, the "chooch" of chooches, was going to make good sound decisions and be free.

I called Sleepy and told her I would see her on Friday to figure out a game plan that she would start the following Monday. Sleepy was good with that, she had a good attitude, and seemed relieved and anxious to get started. I spent the next four days trying to figure out just what the heck we were going to do. I had pretty much used up all the angles of game plans with this kid and I needed to figure out what direction we needed to go. Soon enough it was Friday and I called her to tell her to be home at noon. Sleepy said Ok. I stopped at Mickey D's to pick up some burgers on the way to her house. We sat outside and munched on fries and talked about life.

Sleepy asked me what her plan of action was and I told her I didn't have one. She stared at me with a puzzled look and I told her she had to come up with her own plan. She started in on how many issues she had and she didn't even know where to start. It then struck us both as funny and we laughed for a while. We then settled on some main points just as we had before. Her terms and conditions of Probation were the first priority and main focus. The terms held everything, from attending school regularly to staying drug free. We agreed that if she just followed her terms, all would be OK. We discussed school, working and made short term goals to shoot for. I told Sleepy that being clean from drugs was in my opinion, her biggest challenge. She did agree but quickly changed the conversation. I gave her a hug and wished her luck with her challenges. I told her two things I had learned from my boss... "appreciate your freedom" and "value your life."

A couple of months flew by. Her school was always calling me and she still could not get along with her mom. I tried to offer support and direction, but at times with this "chooch" it was like talking to a brick wall. I remained patient with Sleepy until I found out she had started using drugs again. I blew a gasket. I picked her up at her house and I drove her to her sister's house. I let her know how I felt with several Italian expletives. She knew how upset I was with her and the car became very quiet. When we arrived at her sister's house, she just stayed sitting in the car.

I had a myriad of thoughts running through my head. I remembered the rose in the bed of weeds image and I started to think I had been wrong. Maybe a rose could not grow in a bed of weeds. I was at the end of my rope with Sleepy, but I still was searching for options. I told her I felt I should be done with her, but I would give her one more chance to change her life. Her only option was to come and live in my house with me, my wife and kids. I told her not to mutter a word. I said I was tired of running all over the city, working harder than she did at saving her life. I informed her that it would be very difficult to live in my house. I explained in detail about all of my rules and exactly how it would be. Sleepy was very quiet, and I told her she could respond now, if she cared to. She looked up at me and asked, "How long until I have to let you know?" I answered, "Now". Sleepy said, "Now?" I then told Sleepy that I was done with her and she didn't have to go to my house, but I had achieved my goal to offer her every opportunity to change. The decision was hers and that she needed to tell me before she got out of the car.

In the following moments of silence, I reflected back on all the years working with Sleepy and her family. It was very hard to give her an ultimatum, but it had to be done. Thoughts of our trip to Disneyland, our meals at Mickey D's, the courtroom, Juvenile Hall, her Placements, the yelling fights, the laughter, the tears, everything we had experienced was running through my brain. I felt I was saying goodbye to the "little princess". After a few minutes of complete silence, Sleepy opened the door, and just as I was expecting a thank you or a goodbye, she said, "OK, Mike, but can I move in on Sunday?"

I wasn't sure I heard her correctly so I didn't respond. Sleepy said, "Mike, Sunday, OK?"

"Yea, Sunday will be fine", I said. She closed the door with a smile and I drove away. Then I had a huge conversation with ME. "Holy shit, what did you just do? Did you just open your house up to that kid?" I shook my head, looked at myself in the mirror and laughed. I never thought she would say yes. What was so comical was how I was going to tell my wife that Sleepy was coming to live with us on Sunday.

I settled on the belief that most people wouldn't go the distance with kids like this, let alone move one into your own home. I am saying this wasn't just for Sleepy; it was for me, too. I needed to know I had given her everything I had. I needed some kind of closure with Sleepy.

I pulled into my driveway and just sat in the car. My son came out to ask me why I was just sitting there. I sent him to the backyard fridge for a beer, as if my head wasn't spinning enough. When he came back, I sent him into the house to get his mother. My wife, who I started dating when she was just fifteen years old and had been married to for close to twenty years, walked up to the car and said, "What in the Hell are you doing?" She wore a puzzled smirk on her face, as if she knew something was up.

I just smiled back at her and said, "honey, you are about to have another daughter."

"Whaaattttt?"

"Yea, another daughter, another mouth to feed, take to school, fight with, yell at, and embrace with love, you know, a daughter." I took a sip of my beer, trying to look nonchalant.

My wife's eyeballs were penetrating into mine as she said, "Does this have anything to do with Sleepy?"

"Yep."

"Living here?"

"Yep." I told her Sleepy would be moving in on Sunday. My wife was stunned, so was I. I never thought Sleepy would say yes. I knew she would do better with an upgraded structure and guideline, but I didn't expect myself to follow through with it. I felt a little weird about the whole thing. I had been involved with mentoring kids for years, but for some reason I had become attached to Sleepy, and I couldn't tell you why. I had become close to many of the kids but I had never contemplated having them move in with us. Why had I opened up our lives to this girl? I had no idea where she was going to sleep or how she would get to her school which was fifteen minutes in the opposite direction from where everyone else had to go. My wife and I sat in the backyard and discussed our new situation, and we had to laugh a little. She yelled at me for not discussing this with her before the decision was made but she understood more than any saint would have.

A small part of me even believed that Sleepy wouldn't even show up or call. You never knew what Sleepy was going to do and she didn't know the meaning of consistency.

After talking for about an hour, we decided to buy a bunk bed for our two kids in one bedroom, and we would fix up the third bedroom for Sleepy. We drove to the store and found a good price on a bunk bed and knowing clothes would be an issue, we bought Sleepy a couple of pairs of pants and tops. My wife and I spent Saturday arranging and fixing up the room Sleepy would have. My kids were pretty jazzed because they knew Sleepy and got along well with her, and heck, who doesn't like bunk beds?

Saturday night came and the phone rang. It was Sleepy's mother, thanking me for taking Sleepy in. She couldn't believe it when Sleepy told her. I just told her that I was tired of seeing Sleepy make bad choices and going to jail. We talked for a while and said goodbye. I just hung the phone and it rang again. It was Sleepy. I thought, "OK, this is the 'I am not coming' talk but she told me she would be ready in the morning to be picked up. I was briefly stunned and told her I would be there at 10:00a.m. I hung up and told my wife, "The little princess is coming."

Sunday morning arrived, and I sat sipping my first cup of coffee, staring at the steam rising from the top of the cup. I was hoping for a sign from God that would show me everything was going to be OK, but the sign never appeared. As I made breakfast, I spoke to my kids with more detail about Sleepy and her family life. I wanted them to have a better understanding that they were going to be a big part of Sleepy's rehab team or support squad. They were great and showed their optimistic attitudes. It was time to pick up Sleepy. I drove to Sleepy's sister's house, wondering if I had screwed up. I couldn't help being concerned for my own children. But I was confident my kids were balanced and structured enough that Sleepy couldn't tear them down. I began to feel this was the right decision after all.

Sleepy made bad decisions and smoked pot, but I was sure she wouldn't ask my daughter if she wanted a hit. My daughter and I had discussed this and she felt the same way.

I pulled up in front of the house and Sleepy came outside. Just before she got into the car, I stopped her. I told her this was a big opportunity for her and that it was going to be very strict. I told her if she was ready to take on her challenges and follow my guidelines, then get in and close the door. I said if she wasn't serious about this, then turn around and go back inside her sister's house. Sleepy opened the car door and got in. I looked at her sister who had come out to say goodbye, and she waved and yelled, "Good luck, Mike." I wondered why the sister didn't yell out "good luck, Sleepy." I drove home and not more than two words were spoken. The car was filled with anxiety and uncertainty. I'm sure Sleepy was feeling a little queasy.

We pulled into the driveway and my wife and kids came out to greet us. They helped carry Sleepy's belongings into the house and showed her the room she would stay in. Sleepy sat down on the bed and I walked in and shooed the kids out so I could talk to Sleepy alone. I sat down on the floor and began explaining to Sleepy about the river of life and how sometimes you never knew where the flow would take you. I told her the journey she had been on for so long had had storms and problems, and that maybe that flow wasn't the one she should be on. I spent the next hour going over family values and ethics, and I pointed out the rules of our household and what she could do and could not do.

Sleepy sat very quietly and patiently with little body responses. I could tell as I was speaking to her that this little girl was removed from what she identified with. She was removed from rough people, rough areas, drug use, law violators, crime infected people, and low life lingo. Even as close as we were, I could feel her awkwardness at the situation. I tried to ease the tension by turning on the TV which was in her room, and told her if she wanted to watch

TV late at night, just to keep the volume down low. I explained to her about our school beliefs and how she would not be missing a day. I pointed out that we were a family here; we ate together, played together, and worked together to keep the house clean.... yep chores. I laid it all out on the line and reminded her that she chose to come here. I looked her in the eye and asked her if she still wanted to stay. Sleepy, still not speaking, nodded her head. I felt enough had been said. Sleepy knew what she had to do and that any screw up would result in goodbye. Before I left her room, I turned to her and told her she would be randomly drug tested once a week until I felt certain it wasn't necessary any more. That raised her eyebrows a little and I told her we had zero tolerance for drugs. (Sleepy not only smoked marijuana but had run-ins with meth). I had to be stern on this challenge of hers and I would show no leniency at all. I asked her if she had anything else to ask or talk about. She asked if she could use the phone. I told her the phone was off limits but she could talk to her family. I told her no one could come over and she was not to give out our number. Sleepy didn't like that part at all, but oh, well. The buck stops here and so does her joy rides.

I realized the level of difficulty of removing Sleepy from the wild kingdom of life she lived in and placing her in a stable, consistent family setting. I understood we would have some struggles. I would be open to some of the struggles, but others I would not accept. My goal was for six months. If I could keep her here for that long, I felt we had a good chance of succeeding. I hoped in that amount of time she would gain a different outlook on life and a better attitude. I knew it would be hard for her and Sleepy knew it was going to be hard, too. The last thing I told her was that I was happy she was there with us and I would probably rest better knowing she was safe. She just smiled as if to say, "Thanks for caring."

My wife and I sat in the back yard trying to draft a short plan of action on getting Sleepy to school and so forth. It was going to be a struggle for all of us and it placed more pressure on Sleepy because there would be less tolerance. As my wife began to talk about Sleepy and her needs, I was listening, but my mind wandered off as I thought about Sleepy's father.

Being a father/dad means everything to me. My kids need me so much I just can't imagine how anything could come before them. I guess I wandered too much because I hadn't responded to what my wife had said. I told her what I was thinking and we both just shook our heads.

I have always carried mixed feelings for Sleepy's dad. One side of me hates him for being such a weak man and not standing up for his children. The other side of me pities him for being a drug addict who expects everyone to take care for him. I could remember a few conversations I had with him. He would ask me how Sleepy was doing and I would tell him she was doing drugs and hated school and could use a father. I know it was mean but I was angry with him, and I showed him only the respect I felt he deserved. He did thank me, but I really didn't care then and I don't care now.

I never blamed Sleepy for turning out the way she did. I blamed her for staying that way. My wife had always been a great supporter of this whole "Sleepy" thing. I couldn't have done it without her. I do believe things happen for a reason, and there definitely is a reason I married her. I thanked her for putting up with me and I thought it was so amazing of her to stand with me in supporting Sleepy and having her live with us. How many wives would do that?

Big move here! I hope you do right; Sleepy or you're a done deal. Sleepy lives here! Wow!

CHAPTER 13

A TASTE OF NORMAL LIFE

It didn't take Sleepy long to observe the workings of a stable family. My wife was up getting her clothes ready for work at 6:30 a.m. I prepared breakfast for everyone. All the kids were up getting ready for school and were reminded of what time it was about a zillion times. I had kids from junior college to high school to preschool. I plopped a couple of eggs on a plate and handed it to Sleepy. I told her a good breakfast always insured a good day. She was baggy eyed and confused as if to say, "What am I doing up at this hour?" Sleepy's biggest challenge was that she would be required to attend school every day. I knew the first week would be the hardest but I supported her and cheered her on. I smiled and told her to get used to the madness. Sleepy probably had a ten year habit of going to bed at three or four in the morning and sleeping all day, then waking up with the rest of the vampires at night. It was an acceptable practice for her and would take consistent pushing to change that horrible habit. We made lunches to take if the hot lunches of the day were not desirable. Everyone was ready and we all left at the same time.

I drove Sleepy to school, which was fifteen minute away and gave her money to catch the bus home. We had gone over the routes and Sleepy knew where she had to be and the times she needed to be there. We arrived at the school and I walked in with her and said hello to the teacher. I had worked in the past with this same teacher and knew he would be supportive. I left him my cell number and gave him a brief plan we had Sleepy on. Without collaborating efforts and having a teacher like Mr. Kim, you would never have a chance in taming those wild animals like Sleepy. I was thankful to have him on my side as I drove off feeling pretty good. The music on the radio cheered me and I hoped for a good day.

The day went by pretty fast, and I was anxious to get home to see how Sleepy had made it through the day. Taking three different buses couldn't be much fun. I pulled in the driveway and walked in the house. I could hear the TV on in her room. I was relieved to hear it, but I was hoping it wasn't my son or daughter watching it instead of Sleepy. I knocked on the door and Sleepy was there lying on the bed. Sleepy said she had a good day but the bus ride took forever to get home. I was happy and I told her how proud I was of her. I explained to her that she would soon fall into a routine and it would get easier. Sleepy had homework and she asked me to help her after dinner. My wife arrived home from work and I couldn't wait to give her the big news that of Sleepy went to school and also came home. C'mon, man this is the princess we are talking about here. Going back to the basics means every day counts. After dinner we knocked out the homework and called it a night.

Morning of the second day arrived. I could hear Sleepy's alarm buzzing in her room. I entered her room and woke her up and told her to jump in the shower. She just moaned like a dying cow and covered her head with the blanket. She finally got up, dragged herself to the bathroom and showered. I waited in the truck for a few minutes until she finally came out. She remained very quiet during the ride to school. Fully understanding the change in her habits and lifestyle, I too remained quiet. I didn't think lecturing her or making a big deal out of her slowness that morning would help the situation. Hell, I have had to do that with my own kids. Ultimately, she made it to school no big deal.

I met my wife for lunch and we talked about Sleepy and her morning drag. We discussed waking up a bit earlier and starting the push sooner. That way we could have time to ease her into getting up and avoid the morning bathroom crush. My wife's only problem was Sleepy's letting the alarm go on and on. How could she lie there and just listen to it? We enjoyed our lunch and felt pretty good about Sleepy.

When Sleepy returned home from school, she completed her homework and felt proud of herself. We made it through another day, that's all that mattered.

A week had gone by and Sleepy had done OK. She was going to school, doing homework and doing her chores. Friday came and I had to be at work by 6:00a.m. I took care of the priorities and got a phone call from my wife around 8:30am. She was mad because of a problem she had with Sleepy. She told me the alarm had gone off and she tried to wake Sleepy up but she wouldn't budge. Finally, my wife got fed up and went into Sleepy's room and raised her voice and Sleepy said she didn't feel good. My wife just shook her head and told her she would have to deal with me when I got off work. I hung up pissed off.

About an hour later my phone rang again and it was Sleepy. I asked her about the morning and she said her stomach hurt but then hurriedly told me she had completed her history chapters and would earn five credits when she turned it in on Monday. I just told her we would talk further when I arrived home. That was actually pretty smart of her to call me. She knew she was going to face the gauntlet when I got home. Now all I had to do was to double check her work and verify her story. I finished my shift and spoke with Sleepy when I got home. I told her that I was pretty mad about the "I'm sick" crap and the alarm clock crap. I used some choice words and Italian lingo, and then I double checked her homework. She was telling the truth. She did complete the chapters. I had spoken to her teacher also and he said she was doing fine. He was happy to hear the history book was completed. I told him she would be in school on Monday. I was still mad but I was happy about her first week's work. Overall, it was a pretty good week. She had never completed a book, let alone one full week in school. I was proud of her, and I let her know it. The change would not happen overnight. Good week, dog pound. If you don't know what dog pound means, go to the internet and type in Imolderthandirt.com.

The next week went OK. She had a hard time getting up in the morning and it was a challenge getting her going. One morning she didn't touch the clock when it sounded off and I had to go in her room to turn it off. That morning I had to go repeatedly into her room because she wouldn't move. I pulled her and the covers onto the floor. As I went into the kitchen, I heard her door shut. Some time passed, I didn't hear any movement from here, so I tried her door. It was locked. I yelled for her but she didn't respond so I went into the front yard and looked through the window. Sure enough she was back in bed. I was pissed, so I climbed through the window and dragged her ass to the bathroom. Yes, I climbed through the window of my own house. I turned the shower on and proceeded to throw her butt in when she said, "OK, I'm getting up." I told her she had ten minutes to get ready because she had used up all of her ready time and we were leaving on time. Sleepy got in the truck with her hair still wet. I yelled at her all the way to school. I dropped her off and that was the end of that God damn lazy ass gangster pulling that shit. "You are going to school". That was the worst day of the week for her and she managed to finish another book and received extra credit for a total of fifteen credits in just two weeks. I was proud of her academics but I hated dealing with her in the mornings. I needed some dynamite.

Sleepy had been at our house for two weeks now. She had done really well overall and I was pleased with her progress. She had become accustomed to our lifestyle. She got along well with my kids, did her chores, was doing well in school, and I felt she was headed down the right road. She had also tested clean for drug use five different times. This still didn't support my rose in a bed of weeds theory but I didn't mind. She was doing well and that was all that mattered.

I had to work a late shift on a Friday night and I wouldn't' be home until about 10:00 p.m. I got a call from Sleepy asking if she could go to a friend's house. I didn't know what to say at first. I told her I would call her back. I thought about it for about an hour. I thought about all she had accomplished living with us. I knew she needed to be tested but I felt this was too soon. I decided to call her back and share my concerns with her to see what kind of response I would get back. We talked about being at the house, about school, and being clean from drugs. We talked about responsibilities and actions, and how good she had it now. After speaking to her for a while and hearing her mature comments, I decided to tell her that if she got home before I did, by 10:00pm that she could go. I still wasn't sold on the idea, but what the hell was I supposed to do? She was the one who needed the desire to keep doing well. My wife agreed with me that it was probably too soon, but Sleepy had done so well and she hadn't been allowed to go anywhere, so we let her go. She agreed to be home by 10:00p.m.

I was about to finish my shift about 9:30 when my cell phone rang. It was Sleepy asking if she could stay later. I told her five hours was long enough for the first time out, and that she would be allowed later hours depending on her behavior. I told her I wanted her to come home. I said that if her homework and chores were done during the week, she could see her friend again next Sunday. She said OK, but she wasn't too happy about it.

I arrived home about 10:30, took a shower, and was a little upset because Sleepy was late and she hadn't called. An hour passed and the phone rang. It was Sleepy. The first thing she said was "what would happen if I didn't come home tonight?"

My jaw dropped open, and I was quiet, not believing what I had just heard. Then I softly said, "Your shit would be on the front lawn."

Sleepy then tried to give me a story about why she couldn't make it home. She said she was in Temecula, which was about an hour away and it would take a while to get home.

I said, "Fine, just get home!" I hung up the phone and began a barrage on insults aimed at myself. I was totally pissed off at myself for letting her go. I shouldn't have, and now I could feel bigger problems looming ahead.

At 1:30 a.m., Sleepy walked in the door with a smirk on her face. I didn't say a word; I stood up and placed her drug test piss cup on the table. I turned around and told her to get on it because I was tired and needed to go to bed. She became really angry and couldn't believe I wanted her to test. I knew right away she was dirty and would test positive. I held my ground and all I said was "Piss." She refused and went to her room. I told her, as she walked away, she was not going anywhere, not even school, until she pissed."

Morning came too soon. I called in sick to work to deal with Sleepy. Now comes the funny part...Guess who was up and dressed for school at 6:00am? That's right, the little princess. The girl who had to be dragged out of bed was dressed with hygiene complete. I asked her to pee in the cup and she said she had already gone to the bathroom. I told her to get a glass of water and have a seat.

Sleepy asked, "What about school?"

I told her she wouldn't be going to school until she took the drug test. It was already 6:30 and she needed to be at school by 7:00. I picked up the phone and called her teacher to tell him I needed Sleepy for about an hour and she would be a little late. He was fine with that and told me to bring her whenever it was appropriate.

Sleepy picked up the phone and called her mother, complaining that I wanted to test her. Her mom asked to speak to me. She had the gall to ask me to take Sleepy to school and deal with the test later. I basically responded with "this is my house" comments and I told her if she wanted to make the decisions, Sleepy could go live with her. I was angry and I knew I needed to win this power struggle. Sleepy got back on the phone with her mom but quickly hung up. Evidently she didn't like what her mom was telling her.

I knew she had used meth and she wouldn't come clean by admitting it or taking the test. I looked at Sleepy and told her, "There is no one to call and nowhere to run. Now piss or admit what you did, and we can move forward." We continued to argue as we walked into the backyard. I told her again to admit what she had done, I would take her to school, and we would deal with the consequences later.

Sleepy muttered that she was going back to her sister's house. I wasn't sure I had heard her right so I asked her to repeat it. Sleepy said it again, only louder. I lost it, then. I blew a fuse. I yelled at her, I kicked over chairs and a table, and I broke my favorite coffee cup. I was out of control, I admit it. As I was destroying my patio, Sleepy walked into the house and into her room. I started to follow her, but I held myself back. I couldn't believe her ungrateful attitude and her unwillingness to admit her wrongdoing.

About an hour passed, I had calmed down, and I went to her room. I opened her door and peeked in. Sleepy was gone. I searched the house and the yard. Oh, man, what a rough moment. I hated the entire world, I hated her for using speed, I hated myself for allowing her to go out. I was so angry and upset, I couldn't' function. I had missed work, bought her clothes, fixed up her room, given her spending money, given her my time, and for what? She didn't care. Everyone had told me it wouldn't work and she wouldn't appreciate anything. I had all these thoughts running through my brain and they weighed on me like a ton of bricks. I called my wife and spewed out the entire morning incident and she was angry, too. I just went to lie down; it's all I could do.

Three days passed and I hadn't heard a word from Sleepy. I was worried about her and concerned that she was now making things worse, because that was what she had always done. She was too stubborn to come back and apologize.

I went through each day depressed as Hell. It was my wife who made me realize that all the choices and actions belonged only to Sleepy and we had given her the chance of a lifetime. I knew she was right, but I was in pain and couldn't listen to reason. I had zero tolerance for drugs, especially meth. I would have let Sleepy come back but she would have to surrender the hard core attitude. I was looking for some reason from her, and then I realized she had still been under the influence. Boy, that's where I dropped the ball.

A couple of days later I was sitting in the front yard with my best friend, Jim. He had heard all the stories about Sleepy and had even had some talks with her as well. His wife was in the house with my wife talking about the same thing we were. It was hard to digest all that had happened with Sleepy, and it helped us through it to talk to good friends. Jim had always told me to hold Sleepy accountable for her own actions. As we sat there talking, a car pulled up across the street, and to my surprise, it was Sleepy. She walked up to me and said she had come to get her things and that she was leaving. I didn't even respond. She turned around and walked into the house, got her things, and drove away. Not a word was said during those moments. My wife came out and tried to comfort me by telling me that Sleepy needed me too much in her life, and that she would call. Jim agreed with her. I just sat there, mad, depressed, frustrated, and confused.

Sleepy's mom called to apologize for her daughter's actions. I appreciated the call and told her so.

I felt like I needed therapy. I vented to Jim and his wife that night, my disgust at Sleepy's actions, her parents, and myself for letting her go. It was too much and it had pushed me over the edge that night. But I knew I would be better in a couple of days. You can lead a horse to water ehh.

CHAPTER 14

DAMNED STREET LIFE-AGAIN !

Three weeks had passed since the incident at the house and Sleepy had moved out. I stayed in contact with her teacher at her school just to see what Sleepy ended up doing. I found out Sleepy went to school one day each week. She hadn't completed much work, so after that I didn't bother to call.

The other kids on my caseload gave up info on her all the time. They said she was smoking pot regularly, had started using more meth, and was just partying. I wasn't surprised to hear the bad news. That was Sleepy, but it still hurt me to hear all that.

I was home, telling my wife about all the news I had heard about Sleepy when the phone rang. My wife answered and as she listened, I could see her eyes growing larger by the second. She handed me the phone and told me it was Sleepy.

Sleepy was typically quiet at first, then she told me that she wasn't going to school that much and she knew she needed to do better. I didn't respond. It seemed like she wanted to apologize, to say she was sorry, but she just couldn't do it. With Sleepy, I always had to read between the lines. Just by calling, was her way of saying she was sorry. That's how I took it. I told her that she knew what she needed to do and it was going to take some caring. That was all there was to it. We said goodbye. It was a three minute call.

I don't know if she expected me to ask her to move back or what. She had seemed a little out of it. I was a bit puzzled by the call but I was glad to hear from her. She always reached back to the one thing that was stable in her life. She knew, no matter what she did, I would always listen and try to give some positive feedback, even after I yelled at her. She knew she could call anytime.

About a month passed and we were back to our normal routines at home and work. We had changed the bedroom back to how it had been "BS" – before Sleepy. The kids asked about Sleepy several times, but I just told them I didn't know how she was doing. I couldn't tell them the truth that she was probably smoked out in some run-down house with bodies sleeping everywhere and the smell of low life lingering in the air. I know that sounds terrible, but that is what she had been doing.

My daughter who was old enough to know what was really going on figured it out. She knew Sleepy was out there acting like a fool, working her gang lingo, and drinking it up. My daughter had heard all the events concerning Sleepy and she had talked to Sleepy directly several times about improving her life and how to deal with me. I used to laugh about that. Sleepy would tell me, "Your daughter gave me some insight on how to deal with you." I laughed at both of them.

The whole Sleepy thing bugged my daughter a lot too. She had so much fun with Sleepy at Disneyland that day. Even though they were so different, they did care about one another. Sleepy always asked about my daughter and vice versa.

My cell phone rang one afternoon as I headed for home. It was Sleepy. She was at her sister's house and asked me to stop by. I was in the area so I did. Her sister's kids ran out and gave me a hug, then Sleepy came out. This was the first time I had seen her since she had come back to my house to get her stuff. Her hair was mangy and her pants raked the ground as she walked. I had a flashback of that fourteen year old kid and the first time I met her. In a split second images from past to present flew through my mind. I felt as though we hadn't made any progress. It was a depressing feeling.

Sleepy was quiet for a few minutes then started to mutter. She said she wasn't doing well at all. She said her attendance at school was terrible and she was partying too much and she hadn't seen her PO. That meant she now had a warrant and would be sent to jail if she was picked up.

I just shook my head. I was thinking "15 credits in two weeks and now this." Sleepy said she knew she had it made at my house and finally admitted she had used meth that night. She told me not to blame myself for letting her go, it was all her fault. I appreciated her comments but her current status was like a slap in the face. Then I started feeling sorry for her. I listened to her talk and then I told her I needed to go. I said goodbye and wished her well. Sleepy said goodbye with a puzzled look. I could tell she wasn't done talking, but I was tired and out of patience with her. I drove away with the usual mixed feelings. I arrived home and shared the updated info with my wife. She smiled and kissed me on the cheek saying, "You tried, Babe." Yea, I tried.

I recognized that Sleepy admitting the truth was a positive. I had always been strict with her and she knew at times I was not her friend. I was a true father figure to her in every aspect of that image. I had seen everything she had done, good or bad. Now she was doing badly and she needed to turn things around.

Sleepy would call from time to time and she was always at a different house. I guessed wherever the party spot was would be the place to sleep for the night. I heard she had a boyfriend who was a gang member and also sold and used drugs. I asked her about him and she denied it all. Sleepy was upset that people she knew would give me information and I always knew what she had been doing. She hated that because she couldn't lie about it. I had met her boyfriend before and I knew who he was, just another punk gang member drug addict dealer piece of shit.

He had a bad attitude and I had hoped he would get locked up.

Well the next thing Sleepy told me was that she was pregnant by this guy. I said, "PREGNANT!" I was really mad and I let her know it. I told her she and her boyfriend both had been using drugs and it would affect the baby that she needed to go to a doctor and be truthful about the drug use. Man, the nightmare was getting worse. We had had many talks about relationships, using her sisters as examples, their choices in men and the kind of fathers those men were. I told her to learn from others. What did she do? She picked a man from the sewers. I was shaking my head so much it was about to fall off. I told her that her road just got harder.

Lord, I know you can hear me and I am asking you to help this girl learn responsibility. Show her your wisdom; teach her to be a good mother and to stay clean from drugs. Al I could do was pray – so I did.

What else did I think was going to happen? I should have expected unprotected sex while under the influence. Didn't it go hand in hand? I knew it wasn't the end of the world. Girls get pregnant. They can still go to school; maybe motherhood makes them grow up a little. However, Sleepy couldn't seem to take care of herself, let alone a child. It was the last thing she needed, but maybe it would be a good thing. What the hell did I know? I was scared for the baby because both had been using drugs.

A lot had happened with Sleepy over the last six months. I couldn't even imagine being her. I wondered if her drug use slowed down the rollercoaster life she led or if it just drowned out reality and put responsibility on the back burner.

Looking back at the time Sleepy spent at my house, I realized how hard it had to have been on her. (I know you are saying what!!!) It was like taking a wild animal and putting it in a cage, trying to domesticate it. In Sleepy's case, we were trying to understand why she would rather sleep on a smelly old couch in a room filled with the stench of dope than her own room watching TV. I knew the kind of atmosphere she had been raised in, that she was used to it, and more comfortable there. There had to be a deep pull, a sense of loyalty and respect. In the Mexican gang culture, this is held very high and showing disrespect could get you in a lot of trouble. Living at my house had been out of her comfort zone. That's why my goal had been six months. I thought I could wean her away from her previous lifestyle, but it had been too much for her.

I will always beat myself up for allowing her to go that night, even though Sleepy admitted it had been her fault. I was the grown up and I knew better. Yet I still let it happen.

The reality was that Sleepy, the little princess, was about to become a mother. I knew the day would come, but I had hoped that she would be in better circumstances. I could only hope that she had learned something and would give her baby a better shot at life than she had done for herself. You damn street life, you never give up. God help them.

CHAPTER 15

MOTHERHOOD

Nine months flew by and Sleepy gave birth to a healthy baby boy. I was concerned for the baby from the beginning because of Sleepy's drug issues. Apparently she toned down her usage during pregnancy and her son was fine.

I remember seeing him for the first time. It was weird for me because the baby was pure innocence but had been born to people with so many issues and problems.

I was proud of Sleepy because she didn't use while she was pregnant and I told her so. Her son was a cute kid and I hoped and prayed that Sleepy would care for him more than her mother had cared for her.

Sleepy seemed a little different to me, more mature. Could this be the magic she needed? Could this little guy slow down the train of destruction? I remained hopeful that Sleepy would set a positive example for him. I didn't have any faith in the boyfriend. He was not a real man. He was a bum. A real man takes care of his responsibilities. This guy was irresponsible and a drug dealer and user. He couldn't be counted on at all.

I told Sleepy a hundred times to make self-respect something important. Here's how it works. There are 24 hours in a day. You have sex with a guy for two hours. Yea, it's great, etc., etc. but what about the next 22 hours that are left. That's the part you have to look at. That is the baggage time. Whatever the guy brings to the table—job, character, maturity, responsibility, is what you will be dealing with. You will deal with the baggage more than the sex. This was what I tried to teach Sleepy.

Let's look at boyfriend's resume. He does drugs, sells drugs, won't work, has a bad attitude, is a gang member, has law enforcement issues, yet, Sleepy chose to give herself to him. What the hell are you thinking Sleepy? Why have sex with a guy that is so screwed up? Because Sleepy had the same issues and they thought alike.

I looked down at this beautiful healthy baby and I said to myself, "You don't stand a chance with parents like this." I felt bad for thinking like this but I couldn't help myself. I wish you would have listened Sleepy. Your needs just grew tenfold and boyfriend is not going to help you at all. Your baby boy is beautiful.

After a couple of days in the hospital, Sleepy was able to bring the baby home. She moved into boyfriend's sister's house. My wife and I bought her a bassinet and diapers. She needed so many things. Sleepy also signed up for Welfare so the baby would have the things he needed. I was hoping boyfriend would get serious about work and act more responsibly since he was a father.

Sleepy would get into horrible fights with him. One time they got into a fight and she went after him with big rocks that were in the front yard of some house they were staying at. There were also incidents when she did something to his car because she couldn't catch him. This was the car they depended on.

Sleepy received her first Welfare check and evidently the first one is larger than the average check so that families can take care of their needs in the beginning. The next day I brought Sleepy some baby blankets and other things for the baby. On the floor by the TV was a brand new Playstation game. I looked at Sleepy and she pointed at boyfriend. I asked him, "You bought a Playstation with the Welfare check?" He just looked at me and said that the baby had all that he needed. I felt like hitting him with a shovel. What a bum. I ended yelling at both of them. The attitude of that guy just pushed me to the edge. He just kept playing the game like he deserved it. Rotten bastard, it will catch up to you someday.

Sleepy and boyfriend didn't stay long at his sister's house, maybe three weeks or so. The sister got tired of their fighting and boyfriend started doing drugs with his nephews. Good uncle, huh? It was hard to keep track of Sleepy after they left the sister's house. Weeks would pass and Sleepy would call. They would be at a friend's house and then the next week they would be at boyfriend's grandma's house. They were bouncing all over the place with the baby. I literally screamed at Sleepy to stop dragging that baby everywhere. It was the cold part of the year. One night Sleepy called crying that they had gotten into a fight at a motel where they were staying and the police were called. The police arrested boyfriend on child endangerment charges. I was happy to hear it but felt concern for the baby. Boyfriend had to serve fifteen days in jail, perform community service, and attend anger management classes.

Meanwhile, the baby was growing and his eyes would open wide like E.T. I would get really close to him and say "Phone home." Sleepy would hit me. Sleepy appeared to be a good mother, and I could see the bonding between them. She took him to all of his doctor checkups. Sleepy looked good, happy and the baby were doing great. If we could just cut boyfriend out of the picture, her chances would be better. She had a tough road full of instability and frustration.

I had become an artist at shaking my head. I was a professional head shaker. From all the roads I had traveled with this chooch, I found myself shaking my head more and more. Sleepy still needed to CARE and make better decisions, bottom line. I wished boyfriend had punched a guard and was given life in prison, or he would just move away and disappear. Sleepy showed that when he was out of the picture, she could do just fine.

Sleepy continued to go from house to house, motel to motel. She and boyfriend continued to fight and have problem after problem. They needed to do two things, find jobs and stay clean of any drugs use. I told them this, but it fell on deaf ears.

Boyfriend had grown up in a family with a hard working father who was a respectable man. He had tried to help his son but boyfriend wouldn't stop using drugs and hanging out with gangs. It was a sad situation. Sleepy on the other hand, was doing exactly what her family had done. Sleepy's sisters cared for and loved their families. At times they were good mothers and took care of their children, but at other times they were bad mothers and weren't around for their kids. I expected Sleepy to be the same way.

Her family had all been bad examples. To children growing up observing and learning dysfunctional behavior, it becomes a lifestyle. Being a mother is a big responsibility. A mother needs to be counted on at all times, not just when it's convenient. I believed it was too late for Sleepy to make changes, especially with the man she had chosen. I felt she could be a good mother who nurtures and cares for her son, I felt it was in her, but only time would tell.

When I thought of Sleepy's sisters and what they had gone through, I just shook my head again; living house to house, eviction notices, drug use, joblessness, uneducated, parolees hanging around, law enforcement contacts, and the list goes on. Enough time had passed that I could see youngsters, now teenagers, facing the same challenges as their parents. One of Sleepy's sister's kids was fighting a meth problem and another was having big problems at school. The street life devil was deeply embedded in this family.

Sleepy and boyfriend continued to have major problems. These struggles were not the normal ones you would expect from a couple with a baby. No one was working so no money was coming in, nowhere to stay, doing drugs and drinking, all contributed to the problems. This had become Sleepy's world, not to mention the gang needs and the family dysfunction. It was a sad situation that didn't need to be. These things could have been controlled.

At that point, Sleepy would call just to vent. I had become a small talker, feeling beaten by the street life and its soldiers. Everything I told her seems to come out backwards. I would just listen to her and I could feel her grasping for direction from me, but I just held the phone and gave short responses. "Do the right thing, Sleepy" or "Do what you think is right." This didn't fulfill her need for support and guidance but I didn't know what else to say.

Sleepy had her issues and challenges but as soon as boyfriend would show up, the scene changed. I would hang up the phone after telling her to stare into her son's eye. His eyes held the truth she needed to see, and there was only purity. I told her to ask his eyes what she should do or not do and the answer would come to her. I told Sleepy to be a good mom. Despite the house to house movement, the baby seemed to be healthy and well nourished. My concerns leaned more towards her son and less towards Sleepy.

The answers to the Sleepy saga will be forth coming. Life has a funny way of working things out, but an effort needs to be put forth for it to be productive. I believe that's why the people who make it through are the ones who work hard and stay positive. They remain focused and know the hard times will eventually pass. People who constantly have drama in their lives put forth less of an effort, have a poor work ethic and are therefore pulled into negative circumstances and sad endings. God does help those who help themselves.

If Sleepy had stayed focused and put forth an effort, her life would have been better. I prayed that God would charge into Sleepy's life and boyfriend would get lost in the shuffle and Sleepy would stand strong in the storm. I know I was being selfish because I didn't pray for boyfriend.

Some of my frustrations as a mentor had turned to anger and these were some of the struggles I was fighting. I was close to the situation and therefore easily burned. I lashed out at the people I felt responsible. I didn't like being angry and I wanted to pray for boyfriend but I didn't. I saw no hope in him and I wanted him gone. Most people had seen no hope in Sleepy either, but I continued to hold on.

Sleepy appeared to be a good mother, staying clean and attending to her son's needs. I was proud of her but at the same time, I expected more from her. Sleepy's mom would not take Sleepy and boyfriend in because she had been living with a man who would not allow it. He knew how the family members were; they had stolen from him when he had been trying to help them. Who could blame him? Sleepy's mom helped out when she could but she was usually low on cash so there wasn't much she could do. Her mom also seemed to care more about fixing her own problems than helping any of her kids. She loved Sleepy and wished her well and told Sleepy to work it out. Hold on to being a good mom, Sleepy.

CHAPTER 16

DECISION TIME

S leepy and boyfriend came by the house one night. They needed gas money to get home, so they said. When I first saw Sleepy,
the first thing that flashed through my mind was, she's too skinny
and she's using speed again. She wasn't anorexic but I could tell
she had lost weight. I knew boyfriend had never stopped using but
I wasn't too sure about Sleepy. Her own family told me she was
using and some of my contacts also told me she was. I was almost
sure she was because she looked too frail. I told her she looked
like she either had a severe drug problem or some kind of disease.
Sleepy denied it and attempted to crack jokes. I told her she was
eighteen now with a baby and it was her life she was building.

I talked to boyfriend when Sleepy and the baby went into the
house to speak to my wife. I told him to clean up his act and be a
man. I told him anyone could become a father just by getting a girl
pregnant, but it took someone special to be a dad. I also told him
to get a job. Boyfriend said he wanted to, but he didn't know how
or when. I didn't hear any sincerity in his voice.

I reluctantly gave them money, knowing it might be for drugs
but as God had whispered in my ear over several years, "What they
do is up to them." It's like the bum standing alongside the freeway

with a sign that says, "I'm hungry." I always give them a few bucks and my kids say, "Dad, he's just going to but alcohol." I tell them, "His sign said he needed food. I gave him money for food. If he chooses to buy alcohol, it doesn't affect me. God knows I gave him the money for food." It was the same with Sleepy. You might be saying, "Why didn't you check the gas gauge?" I gave Sleepy a twenty dollar bill and I told her I wouldn't give her another cent until I saw some discipline and improvement towards a better life. I told her if she used the money for anything other than gas or something for the baby, she would have to deal with God about it. Sleepy swore the money was for gas. I hugged Sleepy and wished her well. I prayed that God would guide her to do the right thing. I walked back into the house as they drove away.

My wife couldn't believe after everything Sleepy had gone through, the baby and living at our house that she would even think of coming to the house stoned or under the influence. I wasn't sure Sleepy was under the influence right then, but it was evident that she had been using. I explained to my wife that drugs do that. At first it is fun and games kicking it with your friends. A pipe pops out in the room and everyone takes a hit. You don't want to be left out so you try it. Pretty soon it has you by the tail. Slowly the drug and I'm talking about meth, takes over your brain. You start doing things you would never have done if you didn't smoke it. It controls you and pushes you to want more at any cost. It gives you nerve and it takes away any respect you have for yourself and others. You will hurt everyone around you and your life will be in the sewer. That's why Sleepy and boyfriend could walk up to my door and ask for money. You get an I don't care nerve that displays your character.

A couple of weeks had gone by and I hadn't heard from Sleepy. I knew she received her Welfare check so I assumed the party would be on. She and boyfriend were still jumping from house to house but I wasn't sure where they were. Another week passed and

Sleepy called. She said that the baby was fine but needed milk and diapers. The first thing I thought of was Welfare check and what it had been used for. Sleepy started to cry. She said they were almost to my house and she needed help. I hung up the phone and shook my head. I knew what to expect. For Sleepy to be coming here, every person had to be slamming doors in her face. Sleepy knew she could count on me and come to me as a last resort. At this point I really didn't want her to.

Sleepy and boyfriend drove up and parked in front of the house. Sleepy got out and walked up to the house. Boyfriend stayed in the car with the baby. Before Sleepy could say anything, I told her to bring the baby inside the house. She went, got the baby and came back in. He cried for a little while but a warm bottle soon put him to sleep. Sleepy began to tell me about the problems they were having and she started crying louder. The front door was open and boyfriend was sitting in the car with the windows down. As Sleepy yelled about his drug use and spending the Welfare check on drugs, boyfriend yelled back that he wasn't the only one hitting the pipe. Sleepy got quiet and would barely look at me, let alone speak. I told Sleepy I couldn't believe she had been using and her life was going to fall apart. I said that I was tired of her, boyfriend, and their drug use. I called for my wife and asked her to go to the store and buy diapers, milk, and some things for the baby. She left quickly, knowing I did not want to hand over any more money to drug addicts.

Sleepy began to cry again and withdrew from the conversation. I walked outside to speak to boyfriend. I asked him when he thought he might be pulling his head out of his ass. He was crouched down in the seat with a smirk on his face. He didn't even respond. I told him his drug habit was ruining his life, Sleepy's life and it would surely hurt the baby. I said he needed help and he just nodded his head, not muttering a word.

I walked back into the house and my wife pulled up from the store at the same time. I told Sleepy that boyfriend was totally tweaked out and looked worse than before, and she needed to care about herself and the baby and let boyfriend fall wherever he needed to fall. Sleepy said she just couldn't. I told her, "Then you'll go down with him." I handed her the things for the baby and told her she needed to go. She asked for money for the car but I said no. I walked her outside and she and boyfriend started to argue before she even got to the car. I watched them drive away and I turned to my wife with a look of disappointment and concern. I was afraid for Sleepy and the baby. I agreed with my wife that the baby looked well cared for, clean and healthy.

We talked about Sleepy and boyfriend for the next couple of hours. I told my wife about boyfriend and when I had first met him at the school that Sleepy attended. I remembered that he was a likable young man back then. He was doing OK in school and he was clean cut. He had that gang member look about him, but it wasn't overboard. He wasn't using meth but he was probably smoking weed. I couldn't believe the change in him, how that drug had torn him up. He looked terrible, as if he had a disease or like an AIDS victim. The drug had him in its clutches and if Sleepy didn't pull out, she would be next.

Later that evening, Sleepy called to say she wanted to come by the house and talk. I told her to come on by. It was a quick call and they hadn't been gone that long. Sleepy had moved once again and it was pretty close by. It would only take her five or ten minutes to get to my house. I hung up and told my wife that Sleepy was coming over. We waited, we waited, and we waited. We didn't hear from her and we had plans to go somewhere, so I called Sleepy's niece. She told me that Sleepy was asleep in the back room with boyfriend and the baby. I turned to my wife and told her and we just started to laugh. That was Sleepy, one minute she was coming over to talk, and the next she's a sleeping gangster. We enjoyed our laugh at Sleepy's expense. My wife told me that boyfriend had told Sleepy he was with her only because of the baby. I hadn't heard this before. Now they were sleeping in the same bed together. We started to laugh again. I just shook my head again.

We left for our friends' house and we talked about Sleepy and the baby on the way there. Although the baby's needs were apparently being met, there was more damage being done than just a dirty diaper. He was observing and hearing everything. He was learning their dysfunction and their negative behavior. There was no doubt that their instability, drug use, choice of words, alcohol abuse, and gang lingo would grow on him. He would be the next one in line to carry the torch of destruction. Years later we would discuss his drug use, gang ties, and his family's dysfunction. The generation would continue, street life would claim another victim, one that couldn't fight back. We asked God to fight for him and guide him.

Sometimes things happen for a reason. I had been working with Sleepy and her family for almost five years. It seemed like the more I worked with Sleepy, the more time I ended up spending with her niece Selena. She was always there when I went to check on Sleepy. I would help Selena practice her times tables. If she finished her math and times tables, I would buy her a Chalupa from Taco Bell.

Selena was a nice kid and she was grateful and appreciated things more than Sleepy did. I became really close to Selena and she also needed a father figure in her life. Her dad was never around and she dealt with step-dads or boyfriends most of the time. One summer, Selena spent a month at my house and it was great. She was a loving and respectful kid. She always made sure to thank me and my wife for everything we did. Maybe Selena was the answer I had been looking for. Maybe she was the rose in the bed of weeds. I wasn't sure.

I had mixed emotions about Sleepy being a mother and was still dealing with her drug use and that boyfriend. The longer I thought about Selena, I believed even more that she was the reason I became so involved with Sleepy. Selena went through the same upbringing, in the same house, in the same neighborhood, as Sleepy, yet what a difference. Selena attended school, she acted more mature than Sleepy, and she had fewer problems. I was very proud of her. My only concern was her boyish looks and she seemed to prefer girls. It appeared to me that she was seeking her sexual identity and was exploring all options. I had weekly contacts with her and she trusted me. We could talk about Sleepy and the baby and anything else that came up. We became very close and she became close to my daughter as well. The month she spent at our house bonded them. I always told Selena if she wanted to know what NOT to do, just look at her aunt Sleepy. She just laughed. Maybe you are the reason, Selena, keep doing good. Be that rose in a bed of weeds.

After many hours of deep thought about Sleepy, I made the decision to be the light in her dark world. I prepared myself for the worst. I knew she was still using. I concentrated on Sleepy's needs and continued to guide her, support her, and assist her. I couldn't give up; I wouldn't let that damned street life invade any more. I took my shots, it knocked me down and I almost gave up. I was tired and worn out because nothing was changing. I regrouped and started again with a perseverance I hadn't shown in years. I focused on Sleepy, but also engaged more with Selena. I started to hear a couple things about Selena I didn't care for and I didn't want her to get lost. There was talk of Selena smoking pot, and when confronted she admitted trying it. She also admitted to drinking beer even though I hadn't asked. That was the honesty and respect she gave. Her attitude was good and that made me want to help her even more.

I had always been aware of the odds stacked against Sleepy and her family. I realized that was due to their upbringing. Sleepy and Selena both had strengths and could be productive citizens. They had the ability to learn and grow and be a part of the work force and have enriching lives. I hoped that spending time with us at our home and observing a working stable family impacted their lives in a positive way. I prayed that the desire for a good life would outweigh that street life pull. I kept telling these two girls to dream, dream about their futures.

I believe this is one of the failures in our world today. Kids don't dream any more. Follow this closely; dreams produce a desire which forces motivation, which creates a plan, which forces action which ultimately completes the dream. It can happen and dreams do come true.

With these two girls, it was staying drug free, getting an education, working and having a home, raising kids, being productive, having respect for others, loving God. These were my dreams for them. This is what I wanted to show them and teach them. The question was how badly did they want it? It had to come from them. If they stayed dedicated, then anything was possible. But that damned street life had a hold on Sleepy and wouldn't let go. It had its eye on Selena and was trying to grab her, too. Here comes the cavalry!!

CHAPTER 17

DECISION TIME- AGAIN !

Sleepy and boyfriend continued their ways and fighting with each other. They were kicked out of yet another place and headed for another. They landed at boyfriend's brother's house. This house was known to be a drug/crack house. I remembered Sleepy telling boyfriend she wasn't going there, so it must have been pretty bad if even Sleepy didn't want to live there.

One night Sleepy went to the store to buy milk. She decided to take the car even though she had no driver's license, no insurance, and a warrant out for her arrest. She got pulled over for a cracked windshield (which she did in a fight with boyfriend). The cop ran her name, arrested her, and impounded the car. I received a call from her mom the next day informing me of the situation and asking me to take one of Sleepy's sisters to pick up the baby. Sleepy didn't want to leave the baby with boyfriend at that house. I took the sister to get the baby because I didn't want the baby with that idiot either. The baby looked cute but he had a cold, probably from being dragged around late at night.

The question that came to my mind was why would Sleepy stay with a person she didn't trust enough to take care of his own baby?

I was happy Sleepy had been picked up because I thought the cleanup time would be good for her. She had had a tough week, getting kicked out of two places, fighting with Selena, and being arrested. I always preached, if you do something wrong, it will catch up to you eventually. Well, things caught up to Sleepy. To top it all off, I sent a letter to Sleepy which she got to read in lock-up. It went like this:

Sleepy,

I am working right now and I decided to write you a letter. I have been thinking about a lot of things. You continue to use speed and fail to improve your lifestyle. I can't tell you how disappointed I am in you. You have slapped me in the face more than once, I don't appreciate it, and I am tired of it. At this point, I am frustrated with you and have lost any belief I had in you. This belief is the only thing I ever held onto as you took me down your road of destruction. I believe after all these years; you were shown a better way of life. You were spoken to and taught a better way to live but you continue to choose the other way. I won't give up on you but I'm done with the lectures and extra efforts. I will still be here to guide and direct you and I will remain that stable figure in your life. However, I will not go out of my way as I have in the past. You have burned many people and many bridges in a short time and have burned me enough for me to wash my hands of you, but I won't. I don't want to watch you throw your life away and I don't want to fully close the door on you either.

You also did well picking a gang member drug addict boyfriend to be the father of your baby. I must admit he can be likable but he is headed for prison and you will be left to raise your kids all alone just like your sisters. He won't work, can't stay clean off drugs, and would rather hang out with his homeboys than be with you or his son. You have made your bed with this guy, now you're stuck with him. I would have kicked him to the curb a long time ago but for some odd reason, you like that kind of relationship. I will never understand it, but then again doesn't he supply you with the drugs?

Lastly, I found myself awake on an August morning at 4a.m. I sat down at the computer and started writing about you. The next day I woke up early and continued waking up early each morning and writing more. I wasn't sure what I was doing or why. Now it's late December and I find myself with twenty or so chapters. It's about a fourteen year old girl who meets this Outreach worker and through this relationship, she beats the odds of drugs and gangs and prison and becomes successful. The only problem is the success part. You keep screwing up the ending. So get your act together because I will be finishing soon.

I have nothing else to say to you now. I will be focusing on Selena. I wish you well. I am in much pain these days. There is no question about caring or love. I know I have been like a father to you. I am tired of beating myself up for your failures and continued use of drugs. I will leave you this last thought. I gave you everything I had. I worked as hard as I could to show you that a better way of life was possible. This is true. You are going to be nineteen years old. You can still do the right thing. You need not speak any more words, for your actions will speak loudly and clearly. I ask that you try to set a better example for Selena. She looks up to you and listens to you more than you think. I ask that you make being a mom the most important thing in your life. You will witness your son going down the same road as you if you don't. Reconsider your choice in boyfriend and have some respect for yourself. Get your act together and be responsible. Pray for guidance and strength. Good luck.

Mike

That was it. I don't know how I managed to still feel bad, but I did. After receiving my letter, Sleepy responded back. I was surprised to see that she came across in her letter with an attitude. She stated that she wouldn't bring problems to me anymore and basically said sorry for bothering me. I took it as her not understanding the whole point of it, but whatever.

On Sleepy's ninth day in jail, her baby became very sick. He was having difficulty breathing. It was later determined that he had pneumonia and bacteria in his blood. The doctors were very concerned for him because they felt he should have been brought to the hospital much sooner. They expressed this to boyfriend and Sleepy's sisters.

Sleepy appeared in court the next day and expected the judge to give her the riot act and two more weeks in custody. The judge informed her of her sick son who had been in the hospital for five days and released her to be with him. Sleepy was very upset that no one had told her that her son was sick. Sleepy was happy to be released but was furious at everyone for not telling her. Sleepy didn't call me and I wasn't about to go see her after her letter. But that didn't stop her from calling my wife at work to ask for a ride from the hospital to her sister's house. My wife was stunned but agreed to give Sleepy a ride. They talked about the baby and my letter. My wife tried to explain what my point was but stubborn mule Sleepy just smiled and said she understood. Sleepy said the baby was better but he had to stay in the hospital longer.

A week passed and I hadn't heard from Sleepy at all. My wife and I had finished our day and were settling down to watch the ten o'clock news when the phone rang. Sure enough, it was Sleepy. She was at the hospital and she said she wanted to talk. I was surprised, but I said OK. She vented for a while about the baby, boyfriend, her way of life, and the future. She was concerned for the baby, but not because of health. She thought the hospital was trying to take the baby away from her. She asked if I would come to the hospital and talk to them. At first I told her to ask her mother to do that. She pleaded with me. I told her I would go to the hospital, but I wasn't transporting anyone anywhere, including her. She agreed.

I arrived at the hospital the next day and found the hospital social worker. I spoke to her about Sleepy and the baby. The social worker said the hospital didn't like how sick the baby was when he was admitted and therefore they felt he had been neglected. She said the hospital was taking the routine steps they needed to deal with any type of neglect or abuse. I informed her of Sleepy being in jail and answered more questions. I told her I fully understood and would help in any way I could.

I explained the whole situation to Sleepy. I also exhibited my anger and displeasure that boyfriend and Sleepy's entire family was so stupid they couldn't care for a sick child. I also informed her that she held the total responsibility for her son's safety and health and that her stupid ass had been sitting in jail. I continued to yell at Sleepy and she took it all in without saying a word. She just cried. I also told her that the social worker said the nurses denied some smart ass gang member visitation because he was under the influence. Her being in jail, boyfriend under the influence, and a sick baby are all red flags to educated hospital staff. Sleepy just continued to cry and was not standing her defensive ground. I finished yelling and headed home.

During the last week the baby was in the hospital, Sleepy came to my house and was able to have a nice meal and a hot shower. It gave my wife a chance to talk to her. The baby had been in the hospital for thirty days and Sleepy had been working on finding a shelter she and the baby could go to. Boyfriend had continued his evil ways and Sleepy had finally had enough. We had to have an alternate plan in case the shelter couldn't take her for a while. It was Thursday and the baby was to be released from the hospital on Saturday. I told Sleepy that the shelter didn't have an opening for a couple of weeks so she and the baby could stay with us until they called. Sleepy agreed with the idea and spent Friday night at our house so I could drive her to the hospital to pick up the baby. She would call me in the afternoon when he was released. Saturday evening came, Sunday morning came, and my wife and I didn't know what was going on because no one had called. Monday morning arrived, we went to work, came home, and still no call from Sleepy. My wife called the hospital and was told the baby had been released on Sunday. I tried not to jump to conclusions but I was pissed because idiot Sleepy hadn't bothered to call. My wife was angrier than I was.

At 11pm Monday night, the little princess finally called. She said that boyfriend had shown up on Sunday and they had picked the baby up and gone for a ride. Sleepy said she went to her aunt's house where her father lived. She said she and the baby would be staying there. She said she was sorry for not calling, but she didn't want to bug me. When I asked her about the shelter, she just came up with some sort of bullshit excuse. Out of the blue she said that someone wanted to talk to me. Her father got on the phone and asked me how his daughter was doing. I was stunned for a minute because I hardly ever talked to him. He was clueless. I told him the truth about everything and he just said she had to learn the hard way and thanked me for helping her. I said nothing and he quickly handed the phone to Sleepy. I shook my head and told her, "Good luck. Your boyfriend is a bum and when you decide to call me crying the blues, don't!" She said goodbye and hung up. I told my wife that boyfriend was back in the picture. Another bad decision Sleepy. He had already proven his worth. You should have gone to the shelter, Sleepy.

Another couple of days passed and I spoke to Selena about everything. Selena said she didn't understand her aunt and asked me what my reaction was when I found out Sleepy was pregnant again. Whaaattttt?

Selena said, "You didn't know?" I couldn't believe my ears. Her baby was barely ten months old and she was pregnant again. My wife was going to flip out. Sleepy could have told us while she was staying with us, eating our food, using our shower. Oh my God, I couldn't even breathe when Selena told me and you should have seen the look on my wife's face when I told her.

Selena then informed me that Sleepy got kicked out of her aunt's house and no one knew where they were. They had a reputation of stealing from those who helped them out, so no one would help any more. They probably found another crack house to stay in.

The lifestyle just seemed to get worse and worse. This is how important a father is in a household. Not to say that mothers alone cannot raise their children. But a father who acts like a father can impact a kid's life drastically. I can look back at all the challenged kids I have worked with over the years and I can count on one hand the biological fathers I dealt with. There is a correlation to a problem kid and a fatherless kid. That's why I don't blame the kids.

With a father like Sleepy's, it's no surprise she was the way she was. His comments and concerns may have been sincere, but I had no respect for him and I could have cared less what he had to say. Now, she was pregnant again. Lord, I was shaking my head again. What would it take to turn this girl around? I said some prayers. It was out of my hands or control.

CHAPTER 18

END OF THE ROAD

A couple of weeks had gone by and I hadn't heard from Sleepy. I assumed they had been on the move like they usually were and I didn't know where they landed. I just sat down to watch the nine o'clock news when the phone rang. Sure enough, it was Sleepy.

She was crying and very upset. She told me they had been staying at boyfriend's brother's house, the drug house, and the police had raided it and arrested everyone including boyfriend. I yelled out, "Touchdown!" Sleepy got angry at me but she knew I wanted boyfriend locked up a long time ago. Sleepy even agreed that she was glad he was arrested because it would force him to clean up his act.

The judge gave boyfriend fifty-seven days in jail. I wished it was longer. I always blamed him for introducing Sleepy to speed. He got her to ditch school and to take part in all the negative crap. I knew it had been her decision to participate and I held her responsible, but he was a big part of her down fall. Nevertheless, we all must have self-respect for ourselves.

While boyfriend went off to jail, Sleepy was staying with her cousin in San Bernardino. She was doing OK but the cousin was always on her. He hounded for rent money even though she was broke.

Sleepy came to our house for dinner a couple of times. The first time, we talked about her being pregnant and her not telling us. She said she felt embarrassed and stupid and she knew how hard it was going to be with another baby. Sleepy knew that Selena had told me but she wasn't mad at her. She was happy Selena had told me because I had had time to get over being upset.

During the time boyfriend was in custody, Sleepy handled a lot of business. She made appointments with Welfare and Gain and she checked on her Adult Ed status. I felt she was finally getting into a routine. I dreaded the moment boyfriend would be released because he would bring her down again. She obviously wasn't strong enough to hold her own against him.

I was worn out and needed a refresher. I called my friend Jim and we planned another fishing trip. I brought him up to speed on Sleepy and for some reason we found it funny. All Jim said was, "Pregnant again?" and we cracked up and threw another log on the campfire.

While boyfriend was locked up, Sleepy had a positive attitude and I started to enjoy being around her. We had long talks, shared laughs, and poked fun at one another. I shared my concerns with her about boyfriend and how she would need to stand strong because he would head straight back to the pipe and his ugly lifestyle and expect her to go along. I prepped her for that and made her understand that it was her decision. I wanted her to know that she could control the situation and do the right thing. I told her to stay focused on her goals and she said she understood. But she looked beaten as she said it and we both knew she would go back to him and drama would follow.

Sleepy remained at her cousin's house but they wouldn't help her at all. They wouldn't watch the baby for any reason. When Sleepy had to take an assessment test for school, they wouldn't babysit, so my wife and I did. I guess she had burned them once before so they had no trust in her. Can't say I blame them. At least I had my wife teaming up with me now.

We had Selena over to the house for the weekend. She had gotten in trouble and needed a chewing out. I was glad I was the one to do the chewing. She was smoking pot and drinking and carousing. She wasn't in school but she said she was looking for a job. Some of her comments reminded me of Sleepy when she was eighteen. "I'm going to do this and I'm going to do that." My wife and I gave her a hard time and whenever we commented that she was like Sleepy in any way, Selena would blow a gasket. She did not want to be placed in the same arena as Sleepy even though her actions were beginning to emulate Sleepy's. She would party until the wee hours, smoking pot, no school, no job, and staying from house to house. The pattern was clear and the handwriting was on the wall.

We talked about Sleepy and the baby and the one on the way. Selena was mad at Sleepy for being in jail when the baby got so sick. Selena had a hard time dealing with Sleepy and boyfriend. But I asked her to try harder to get along with Sleepy and to offer help and support. Selena had a mothering instinct, which I'm sure she learned from having to fend for herself while growing up. Selena had younger siblings and was the one who provided the care since her mother only wanted to party. Selena was basically raised by her grandma. Actually, Sleepy's mother was a better mother to her grandchild, Selena, than she was to Sleepy.

I told Selena I was happy boyfriend was in jail and she agreed with me. She didn't want him getting out either.

Selena was always a good listener. She was more sincere and cared more than Sleepy, and she listened to and respected my wife and me. I was glad to spend time with her and she loved hanging out with my daughter. They got along great and I never worried about Selena asking my daughter if she wanted to get high or any other negative approaches.

We had a nice dinner and I dropped Selena off at her aunt's house, (Sleepy's sister). There were four kids playing in the half dirt-half-grass front yard. I drove away thinking of their chances and the generational pull of their negative lifestyles. I prayed for their futures. I could almost see that street life devil waiting around the fence to grab its next victim.

I know God knows all. I do have faith, I just wonder why things happen the way they do. I believe we empower ourselves and I believe things happen for a reason. Did I come into Sleepy's life or did she come into mine? Am I teaching her or is she teaching me? Is she the sacrificial lamb so I may learn about troubled families, placement, drug and law enforcement issues, homelessness, outreach programs, shelters, welfare and gain, unemployment? Is Selena the reason I met Sleepy? Sleepy and Selena both now have a father figure in their lives. I hope to learn from all of this and I am much stronger, wiser, and more focused on the next kid that I work with. I will always believe that God's hand was in this, and even if Sleepy is not doing well, I will still smile and push her a little harder than before.

I believe we should not question faith. I will continue on the path I have been shown and continue doing what I can to direct and guide Sleepy and her family.

CHAPTER 19
RELEASE TIME

Sleepy was still living at her cousin's house. They really didn't get along and I was confused as to why they even let her move in. They were probably in it for themselves to get a piece of that Welfare check more so than to help out a family member. If that wasn't bad enough, boyfriend's fifty-seven days was cut by two days and he was now living at his grandma's house. He first called me on the phone and asked where Sleepy was. I told him she was at her cousin's house but I didn't have the number and didn't know how to get a hold of her. I wasn't motivated to do so anyway. We talked for a short time and he informed me about his time in jail and oh, yea, how he found God. Could this be true and God was going to turn boyfriend's life around? Could it happen, yeah? Was it going to happen to this guy? I think not. I was in no hurry to assist him in getting back with Sleepy, who he didn't take care of and his son, who he didn't even know. The longer I could keep Mr. Meth-breath away from them, the better. I was filled with pessimism because I knew how weak Sleepy was. A place to live would be their problem. Sleepy's cousin was in the process of kicking Sleepy out when boyfriend was released. They sure wouldn't let boyfriend into their house. Sleepy and boyfriend had burned their bridges and really had no place to go. I knew they weren't coming to my house and Sleepy didn't ask. Sorry, Sleepy, but you had your opportunity and you blew it. Now it's on you. You can ask and you probably will but you are not coming here. Bunk Bed avenue is not here anymore.

Once boyfriend was released, it didn't take long for my phone to ring again. I turned over in bed and saw that it was 12:30am. I just about crapped because everyone knows not to call me after ten. I picked up the phone, half asleep and managed to ask who it was on the phone. Sleepy said it was her and her cousin had kicked her and the baby out and they were at the corner market and they needed a ride. I was still half asleep and she had to repeat the whole story over again. Boyfriend had been dropped off at Sleepy's cousin's house and three hours later they all started arguing and the next thing you knew, they were at the market calling me. It took boyfriend just three hours to upset the household. I just started laughing and told Sleepy good luck. Sleepy reminded me about the baby and how cold it was outside. I got pissed off and yelled at her but it didn't diminish the fact that the baby needed to be inside and out of the rain. I hung up and got dressed as my wife asked me about the call. She just shook her head. I told my wife if Sleepy didn't have the baby, I would let her and boyfriend stand in the rain all night.

Sleepy and boyfriend needed a ride to his grandma's house. It wasn't close by either. I did ask Sleepy if she had called her mom or her sisters. She said she couldn't count on any of them. I didn't have a response because it was true. I arrived at the corner market and I couldn't believe my eyes. There were people everywhere; crack heads, prostitutes, bums lying around with bottles clutched in their fingers. There were people sitting in cars and walking around like they were on a Sunday stroll. I looked in a donut shop and there they were; Sleepy boyfriend, and the baby. They spotted me and raced for my truck. I helped put the stroller in the back as they buckled up and off we went. Sleepy quickly thanked me for picking them up. Boyfriend thanked me too. In fact, he never stopped talking during the entire ride to his grandma's. He told me he was tired of everything and sick of needing to depend on everyone. He said he had a job lined up and would follow up on it on Monday. He also said that this time in jail was different and spoke about finding God. He said he was looking forward to a new life with his family. I wished him luck and handed him a Drug and Alcohol counselor's business card. I explained how much help he would need to overcome his challenges and drug use. I told him my friend could help him. He took the card and put it in his wallet. Could this really be a turning point for boyfriend? I didn't know but I wouldn't bet on it.

We arrived at boyfriend's grandma's house after a twenty minute ride. Sleepy and boyfriend got out and gathered their things and the baby from the truck. Sleepy thanked me again and seemed truly grateful. I reminded her to stay focused on her life and that would impact her son's life, but she couldn't help boyfriend, he had to help himself. Sleepy said she knew and told me to be careful on the drive home. I pulled away telling her to say her prayers. I had a thousand questions running through my mind about this new Sleepy caper. Would boyfriend keep his word? Would Sleepy keep hers and stay focused?

I thought about Sleepy all the way home. I thought about how hard it was going to be to establish a normal routine and level of comfort; owning your own car, having your own home, ordering pizza on a Friday night. I thought about boyfriend and his drug addiction. Sleepy had done well in staying clean but boyfriend had stopped only because he had been locked up. The bigger question was, if he smoked pot again, would Sleepy smoke with him? If he used meth, would Sleepy use with him? They went hand in hand when it came to drugs. It was hard to fight it when the one you cared about wanted to do it. At that point in their lives, you would think they would do whatever it took to do the right thing. I had given boyfriend the phone number of my friend the drug counselor. They should be calling him the next day. He would give them the direction they needed. Would they call? Probably not. I didn't have any answers but I knew if they used again, their lives would change forever and the turmoil would start again. Anything would be possible if they stayed clean.

The weekend came and I got two phone calls back to back. The first was from Selena and had heard through the grapevine that Sleepy had moved and boyfriend was out. I had already heard and gave her a play by play from the phone call at 12:30 am. She always enjoyed my antics when I spoke like Sleepy and boyfriend. We shared a good laugh and then spoke about some more serious things. Selena had been drinking and hanging out with her friends. She played everything down and tried to make me think she was in control. I didn't though. I knew everything was not OK. Selena was out there fooling around and so far had been lucky. I told her to calm down and to get a job and go to school. She gave me all the answers she knew I wanted to hear.

The next call was from Maria, Sleepy's sister. I hadn't talked to her in a while and when we did talk, we covered everything and it usually took an hour or so. She laughed about the newest on Sleepy and boyfriend. We talked on and she told me about her ex and how he lived and worked out of state and never sent any money home for the kids. They always argued whenever they talked and he still wouldn't send any money. It was the same story, just a different sister.

I was proud of Maria though. She seemed to want more out of life. She knew she had to work, but she didn't know what to do. One day she called and said she had an interview with a major grocery store chain. I was amazed that she did this on her own, but she said she didn't have anything to wear. I told her to get a ride to my house and I would help her. I thought that alone would stop her but she found the ride. Sometimes a small challenge is good to see how serious a person is. Maria could find a ride to a concert two hundred miles away. If she was serious about a job, she could surely find a ride to my house. We went shopping and bought the clothes she would wear if she worked there. She got the job and was very excited. I rode that happy wave as long as I could. It was not easy getting any happiness from this family. I praised her and we talked about the impact the job would have on her and her kids. Her other family members were very envious of her. It wasn't too long until Selena found a job and we celebrated that, too.

The last reference to Sleepy's brother, Midnight, had him on parole just finishing a total of six years in prison. I must admit I had forgotten about him with all the havoc going on with "the girls." I just hadn't had a reason to think about him. I had recently talked to him and learned he got off parole and was working, staying clean, and even mentoring youth in the community. I was blown away by this man and was happy to hear he turned his life around. It was a joy to talk with him and it gave me hope for Sleepy. I felt the family was doing better, finally. Maria had a job, Midnight was doing well, and boyfriend was still clean, as far as I knew. I talked to the family about consistency and working together. I asked the family to help Sleepy and talk to her about her life and making good choices. A breath of fresh air for now.

CHAPTER 20

DRUGS AND PREGNANCY

Months flew by and Sleepy looked like she had a basketball tucked under her shirt. I only saw her once, but I managed to talk to her on the phone maybe twice a month. I encouraged her to take care of herself and to see her doctor. She said she would and that she was doing OK. I told Sleepy that I had heard boyfriend was using again and he wasn't doing any good. She said he had started using and they had been fighting a lot. I told her to leave him and go to her sister's house. She declined. I told her good luck.

It wasn't too long after that when I received a phone call from Sleepy's mom that Sleepy had given birth to a four pound baby girl. I was surprised that the baby weighed only four pounds. Her mom then dropped a bomb on me. She told me the baby had traces of methamphetamine in her blood and the hospital secured her in a private room. The police and social workers were involved. I was silent, I couldn't say anything. Sleepy's mom asked me if I heard what she had said. My only response was, "Yea." Sleepy's mom started to cry and I asked her if there was anything else I needed to know. She said no and I hung up. My wife walked into the room and she saw the look on my face. I told her about the phone call and it was the angriest we had ever been since meeting Sleepy. We had no sympathy any longer, no empathy or compassion. We wanted justice.

I felt for Sleepy's daughter who had been born to two selfish people who had abused her that way. The phone rang gain and it was Selena, crying about the baby. I told her to look at what drugs do and to learn from it. Selena hated Sleepy for what she had done and she was afraid for the baby. I found out through more phone calls that the police went to the residence with CPS workers and took Sleepy's son as well. The two kids were no longer in Sleepy and boyfriend's care and they would both have to appear in court at a later date.

Sleepy was released from the hospital and was not heard from. No one really knew what was going on. I would get phone calls from Selena or Maria and they would tell me that Sleepy was with boyfriend probably doing drugs, going from place to place. I got used to being disappointed with that girl. What was so sad was that it didn't need to happen.

One night Sleepy did call me. We talked about the baby and meth use. She wasn't crying or being dramatic. Then she asked me for fourteen dollars to help pay for a room. I told her she made me sick to my stomach just talking to her and I hung up. She didn't call back so I guess she figured out she wasn't getting any help from me.

My wife and I talked for hours after that. We just couldn't believe Sleepy used during her pregnancy. That poor baby having that shit running through her veins, no choice on her part but to take in what her mother gave her. Sleepy told me she was taking some kind of medicine. She didn't say what kind. What a liar. I was glad foster care had taken the children from her. I knew Sleepy and boyfriend's good time was about to come to an end. Their court date was the next date and I was confident the judge would be hard on them due to their past records. The court date arrived but Sleepy was the only one who showed up. The judge ordered both Sleepy and boyfriend to treatment. I spoke to Sleepy afterwards and she told me she was working on an arrangement to have boyfriend's parents take over guardianship of the kids. I didn't say much and I left. Sleepy knew it was the last straw when I didn't have anything positive or hopeful to say. She didn't deserve squat.

At the same time all of this was going on, Selena drove up to my house in a small black car with two of her friends. She was driving with no license. I gave her a hard time for driving and I asked her whose car it was. She told me it was her friend's car and she had been driving it for two weeks. I yelled at her for a while, we talked about Sleepy, and then she left. It was good to see Selena but I didn't like her driving.

The following week, the parents of the girl whose car Selena had been driving called the police to report it stolen. Selena didn't know this. She was out drinking with her friends and driving around and got stopped by the police. She was arrested for DUI and grand theft auto. They took her to jail. She called me, crying, asking me for help. I just told her I was sorry and I laughed and said "Good luck." I also told her I would not accept any more phone calls and I wished her well. She was upset with me but what could I tell her? She didn't think of me or need me when she was out there tearing up the road. She swore to me that the girlfriend who owned the car told her parents that she let Selena take the car. The parents didn't care because Selena never brought the car back. What an idiot kid.

Selena was ordered restitution and DUI classes. I talked to her about her drinking and how she needed to be more responsible. Because Selena didn't use meth, it was almost accepted that she drank or smoked pot. At least she wasn't totally like Sleepy. Selena wasn't the most responsible girl even though she worked several different jobs. She ended up blowing off all the court directives for classes and restitution and she ended up back in court. They barely let her walk out of the courtroom that day and she had to do fifteen weekends in jail starting the following week. Selena didn't even know how to get to the jail, let alone do fifteen weekends. I knew when she told me about it, she probably wouldn't show up for even one weekend. She wasn't serious about doing the right thing and I was worried about her.

Sleepy was still hanging out with boyfriend. They jumped from house to house, probably sharing the same pipe. I had heard several different things, but I didn't know what to believe. One person told me she was shooting meth with a needle instead of smoking it. I was hoping that wasn't true, but with Sleepy, anything was possible. It appeared that Sleepy was falling to the bottom and there was no stopping it. Sleepy didn't just wake up one morning and start using meth. She didn't just wake up one morning and she was a gang member. These were learned behaviors. Sleepy's sisters had daughters that threw kegger parties for them when they were fourteen. They thought it was OK for them to drink as long as they were home. That's how they lived. I didn't agree with it but that's how they were raised.

No one touched meth until boyfriend started coming around. Meth had a hold on Sleepy and she couldn't do anything about it.

In defense of the family, I don't think any of them did drugs while they were pregnant. Sleepy stood alone on that one. When I confronted her about it, she said she didn't know she was pregnant. True or not, I no longer wanted to do shit for her.

Sleepy did ask for some assistance in getting her kids back. I told Sleepy if she went to treatment, my wife and I would attend meetings as her support cast. She was thankful, but that is all I would do. Meetings were once a week and she was happy we agreed to support her. Now we would see if she was serious about getting help.

People that I hadn't seen for a while would ask about Sleepy and I would just look at my wife, smile, and tell them, "Let's talk about something else."

CHAPTER 21

RECOVERY

With her kids in the adoption system, Sleepy started the treatment program. It was a live-in placement with strict guidelines. She had to really watch what she said or did, because any mess up would be a violation of a court order. The placement was designed to work with one's drug issues, self-esteem, and parenting skills. If Sleepy was there long enough, her kids would be brought in to live with her. Drug free reunification was the goal.

Sleepy was lucky they accepted her, but she wasn't too happy to be there. Sleepy had asked us to be her support group and we agreed, so we had to attend meetings. She had also asked her mother and Selena, and they attended, too. I didn't mind helping in this way if Sleepy was going to be in a program. After the support classes we scheduled a day on the weekend to go to see Sleepy. She didn't look so good. She looked very tired and run down. She seemed to have low tolerance and seemed to be mad at everyone around her. She had been in for almost a month so I felt she was clean. Maybe it was the drug she wanted and couldn't have and that was what made her irritable. Our first conversation with her was about her children. Sleepy expressed negative comments about the system and how CPS had stolen her kids from her.

I reminded her of a drugged up dad who hadn't even shown up for court for his kids and a mom who had chosen a needle instead of holding her daughter. I also told her if she wasn't going to give her kids a chance for a better life, then maybe they were better off with someone else. She gave me a mean look and then began to cry. I ended up becoming angrier and told her we wouldn't be sitting there if she had stayed focused on goals and had stood strong against boyfriend and or drugs. Then I told her to quit her crying because it wasn't going to change anything. Her kids were the ones suffering from her actions and she was sitting there in a court ordered rehab blaming the system. She didn't say much after that. My wife muttered a couple of things to Sleepy but she didn't even respond. I got up from the table and told my wife to get up too. I turned to Sleepy and told her to find herself and get rid of that selfish, ungrateful drug using demon girl that sat before us. As we walked away, Sleepy started to cry more and walked to her room. My wife and I left. We were pretty upset. We talked on the drive home. We agreed that it was a process that perhaps we didn't understand. We had never dealt with a drug addict before so the impacts and effects were new to us. We weren't ready for her bad attitude but I still felt I had said and done the appropriate things. Whenever I worked with any kid who was in trouble, I always looked for that one word, accountability. Sleepy didn't have it and that's what pissed me off. It didn't help calling her names at the end of the visit, but it made me feel a hell of a lot better.

It was hard for me to let go of the fact that Sleepy had used during her pregnancy. It lingered in my mind night after night. Her baby girl had breathing problems, but was getting better. We didn't get a lot of information about Sleepy's kids, but we did hear that they were OK.

I sat in my backyard with my friend Jim and gave him yet another update on Sleepy. I told him about the baby's problems and Sleepy's treatment program. All he could do was shake his head.

It wasn't a laughing matter, but what else could we do, what else could happen in the Sleepy drama. We laughed because she had done just about everything short of robbing a bank. I felt beaten by that damned street life and laughing was all I had left. It was either laugh, or cry.

Sleepy had been in recovery for eight weeks. The social worker told her she could have her kids with her the following week if she continued to do OK in the program. My wife and I drove out the following weekend. Sleepy had her one year old son and her baby daughter. It was great to see her with them. Her son acted like he hadn't forgotten her. He was very cute with big eyes. Sleepy's daughter was tiny and she had a cold and we could tell she was uncomfortable. I couldn't help but blame the drug use on the baby's cold and sniffles and sneezes.

Sleepy had only a brief moment with her daughter after birth. As soon as the hospital detected drugs in her bloodstream, they whisked her away from Sleepy. This was the first time Sleepy had been able to hold her, bathe her, and comfort her.

Her son was full of energy. He was walking and wanted to play. Sleepy was on the move with both kids and she had her hands full. I just watched as I sat at the table, smiling. Sleepy looked at me and told me to shut up in a loving way.

The kids finally went to sleep and it gave my wife and me a chance to talk to Sleepy. She told us that she had gotten into it with another girl in the program three days earlier. She said they were fighting and they had to be separated. Sleepy was placed on contract. If she violated he contract in any way, she would be terminated from the program. If this happened, the social worker would take the kids back to foster care.

This unique program taught independence and responsibility. It allowed one to leave the facility and take care of business, such as court dates, doctor's appointments, etc. It was a good program and Sleepy was now on contract with no wiggle room.

I felt I was just going through the motions while I talked to Sleepy. I still cared but I was so burnt out, I was numb. I couldn't get excited, upset, happy, or sad. I hoped to be proud of my little girl someday, but I didn't think it would be anytime soon.

One day I received a letter from Sleepy. She had written a poem:

Hello, it's me again writing these few words down your way, to wish you guys good days and wonderful nights. I wrote a poem for you as well. Well, thank you again for everything. I promise I will show you both in my completion of this program and getting rid of that old Sleepy. There just isn't any turning back anymore. For me, it's looking forward with the children I was blessed with. Well, I hope you enjoy my poem. See you next week. Take care and thanks for caring. With much love and respect, always your lil' girl, Sleepy,

P.S. You were all a blessing from God alone to me and became a shadow always being by my side. You have made a difference in my life. Without you, I would be a lost child, and I hate to say this, but dead. Somewhere, if it wasn't for you, "you have saved my life" and "my children's." I'll never forget you all.

I am sorry

I know I wasn't there but deep down inside I really care
I might not have shown you all my love; my life has been a struggle and sometimes a shove
I'm sorry if I caused any hurt or pain, responsibility of many
And each day a gain
I tried my best to be there for you; forever you will be inside my heart
You've been there for me right from the start
Sleepy
Dedicated to the ones I hurt and forgot about in my addiction
I love you

I received this and, yea it helped to know she at least thought about things. I didn't change the fact that she was in a recovery program and was about three years behind in maturity. It did show some love and recognition for the people who truly cared about her. The way I interpreted this was the "I'm sorry" part was directed to her children and the dedication part was for me. I could be wrong.

Sleepy had been doing OK in the program. She was with her kids and learning to be a mom. She had some problems with time management, especially when she left the facility and returned at a later time than she was supposed to. She always came back clean, but she was always late. I guess this occurred more than we knew.

One of her friends from the neighborhood died and she was allowed to go to the funeral services. She returned to the facility late and was talked to and written up for it. She couldn't understand the impact of the program, that following instructions and adhering to program rules was what it was all about. The last talk I had with her reinforced what staff at the program had been working on with her. A responsible, punctual, caring mother was the goal and when one faltered at achieving this, there were consequences. Timing was, and always will be everything.

Two days later, Sleepy's dad died. He was at Sleepy's sister's house, sitting on the sofa. He hadn't done anything different, alcohol and heroin, what he had done for years. No one realized he was dead. Life was going on as usual around him, kids sitting beside him on the sofa watching cartoons, people walking in and out. One guy who drank with him asked him a question and when he didn't answer, they started to look more closely at him and noticed the stiffness. They were shocked that he died right there on the couch. They said it was an overdose. No surprise there.

I didn't know how to feel. I was angry with him because he let his family down. It was hard on Sleepy because she had always defended him and held on to the belief that he was a good dad. I talked to Sleepy about her dad and the car wash they were holding to help pay for the funeral.

The program was allowing Sleepy to attend the car wash and the funeral, but with strict guidelines. She was allowed two hours at the car wash, which didn't make her happy. Sleepy went to the car wash the following day but didn't return to the facility until three hours later. Staff was not happy with her. They called her onto the office and spoke to her about being late. Sleepy reminded them that it was her dad they were talking about. Staff became angrier. They told Sleepy that she would be given two hours for the funeral and could not attend the gathering afterwards at her family's house. This infuriated Sleepy and she got into a yelling match with staff and supervisors. The yelling match escalated into verbal commands which Sleepy refused to follow and then was followed with a threat of discharging Sleepy from the program. Sleepy lost control. They discharged her from the program. Sleepy called me crying and told me she would be leaving the program the next day. Destination was unknown.

The social worker was called and she took Sleepy's kids back to temporary foster care parents. I spoke to the Social Worker about Sleepy's discharge and we were both upset. I decided to go to the facility to speak to a supervisor. They wouldn't give me much information but I showed my displeasure with the way they handled Sleepy. I told them they took the easy way out. I understood that Sleepy needed to follow the rules, but I felt they chose the wrong time to play hardball. Sleepy's friend had died, her dad had died, and she was overwrought and vulnerable. I felt they should have waited to confront her until she had calmed down a little. And none of us on her support team had been called in to help or give our opinions as to the best way to handle the situation. Sleepy was only human. Why do we have support teams? Why put people through becoming teams if we can't be there during crunch time?

The program had been in service for years. With their experi-ence, I felt they should have handled it better. I knew what a pain in the ass Sleepy was. I knew she was never back on time, but she was still clean. She had mouthed off and disrespected staff, but Sleepy had only three weeks left in the program. I told the super-visor they should use the support teams before any termination. She said she would bring it up at the next staff meeting. I walked away. Too little, too late.

Sleepy was upset and crying on the phone to me. She told me she would be going to her sister's house. The social worker told her she needed to attend NA meetings and start an out-patient program right away. The social worker gave her a court date and said Sleepy needed to be there. It would look good to the judge if Sleepy was attending meetings and enrolled in an out-patient program.

I supported her and told her not to give up. I told her to think about her children and to focus on the things she needed to do. This was indeed a tough time for Sleepy and I saw it as a turning point for her. I continued to remind myself of all the opportuni-ties Sleepy had over the years. All of this was a result of her actions and bad choices. Now she needed to buckle down and take charge of her life.

I tried to be optimistic, but it was too hard. Back to foster care, back to court, back to her sister's. Where was boyfriend during all this turmoil? Probably smoked out somewhere, doing what he did best, drugs, drugs, and drugs. I heard they had seen each other while Sleepy was in the program. I didn't ask. I was afraid for Sleepy and was preparing myself for another one of her street life runs. I didn't trust her and knew her patterns.

It was time to get her into an out-patient program, Hey, Sleepy, how bad do you want your kids back?

CHAPTER 22

THE LAST STRAW

Sleepy was staying at her sister's house and then I heard she was picked up by boyfriend. Maria and Selena were mad at Sleepy because her kids were taken by CPS. There was no sister or aunt love or loyalty and Maria and Selena felt free to be honest and tell me everything Sleepy was doing. I felt Sleepy didn't have anything to care about and she would give it all up. I contacted her social worker who cared about Sleepy and her family. She told me that Sleepy attended two NA classes and signed up for an out-patient program but hadn't been seen or heard from in over two weeks. I was pretty disgusted but not surprised. I hadn't heard from her either.

About three more weeks went by and everything was quiet. I hadn't talked to anyone. It was actually nice but at the same time I had visions of Sleepy out there smoking weed, doing meth, drinking and just throwing her life away. It was hard for me to shake her off totally.

One evening we were having dinner when the phone rang. It was Selena. She told me Sleepy and boyfriend got arrested and were in jail. She said they were arrested for drugs on person, under the influence of a controlled substance and grand theft auto.

I was pleased that the party was over and those selfish idiots were in jail. I knew the consequences were going to be severe because they both had juvenile and adult records. I had always been able to help Sleepy in a pinch but this time it was different. There was nothing I could do even if I wanted to.

Court and sentencing came quickly and Sleepy was given three years in state prison. After several more court dates, her sentence was reduced by her admitting her crime and she agreed to take one strike. This was serious stuff and the judge told her that any other involvement in crime or failure with probation or parole would put her in prison for the remainder of time. Sleepy left the courtroom in shackles headed for Banning Road Camp where she would start her one year sentence.

I was upset and felt like a failure but my wife, as usual reassured me that we did everything humanly possible to save this girl. Selena and Maria were upset and crying over the whole thing and were mad at Sleepy, but I challenged them on their own shortcomings and asked them if they had any room to talk. Maria quickly retorted that at least she still had her kids. I replied back, "You mean the ones that hardly ever go to school?" We were all upset and now attacking each other. I gave them both hugs and went home.

I went back to my daily grind and used Sleepy as an example to remind Selena how she had better improve her efforts or she would be following in her aunt's footsteps.

I took calls from Sleepy from time to time and we would have a brief talk. It was hard for her to call me and equally hard for me to take it. I was just there, barely communicative, not supportive or optimistic. Every once in a while I would receive a letter from Sleepy and I did write her back, but only a few times. She asked me several times to put money on her books and send her stamps. I sent her the stamps but that was it. Throughout the next eight months, Sleepy asked me to drive to Banning to see her. It was only twenty five minutes away, but I never did. She knew I didn't want to see her. I accepted her collect calls because her family wouldn't or couldn't because of the cost. She always wanted to hear about her family and any gossip concerning her niece. I really didn't even like paying for the collect calls, but I couldn't shut the door totally on her. I continued to work with Maria and Selena.

Before we knew it, ten months had gone by and we were anxiously awaiting Sleepy's return to civilization. For the last couple of months in our conversations, Sleepy would bring up where she would be going when she was released. I know she was afraid and unsure or at least that's how she sounded.

She did receive the good news that the foster parents of her kids would not be allowed to adopt because they only wanted the boy and not both of the children. The social worker said the children would not be split up. Whoever adopted them had to take both of them. The foster parents stepped out of the picture and Sleepy's kids were placed in a different temporary housing. According to the social worker, this allowed a window of opportunity for Sleepy to come back into the picture. There was a slight chance if Sleepy got out, started a program, exhibited good behavior, the social worker would go to court and ask the judge to consider allowing the kids back with Sleepy. That's all Sleepy could talk about. Her attitude was optimistic and her outlook on life improved.

Our next topic of conversation was where she was going to stay when she got out. Sleepy wanted to try living at my house again, but I told her I would have to think about it but in no way would I be in favor of having her and her kids. Sleepy understood that it would be temporary.

Sleepy's social worker helped me with a short plan of action that would allow time for Sleepy to find housing, get her kids back, and be on her own. I was OK with the temporary thought. There was no way I was going to care for her kids while she was out blowing smoke with boyfriend.

In fact boyfriend had only done a short stint in jail, and I heard he was back at it worse than before. He would never be coming to my house again!

I really didn't want Sleepy living with us but with the social worker's support we might be in for two weeks to a month. I figured I could do that. I spoke to Sleepy about all of this and she felt it was too good to be true. I couldn't believe the look on Jim's face when I told him that Sleepy was going to live with us again.

Another two weeks went by, it was Sunday night and I hadn't heard from Sleepy. I assumed all was OK and I figured she hadn't called because I got on about calling too much. About eight o'clock the phone rang and my wife answered it. She whispered to me that the machine said Riverside detention Center. I assumed that Sleepy must be getting released and the inmates had been moved from Banning to Riverside. My heart raced a bit realizing that Sleepy would be sleeping on my couch in a few hours. I said hello and was shocked that Sleepy was crying and could barely speak. I asked what was going on. Her next words knocked me on my ass.

Sleepy, in her muffled voice, told me she was given and early release on Friday. (Early release?) She kept crying. I asked her why she was in a Riverside jail on Sunday when she was released on Friday. What happened? She told me her mother picked her up in Banning and dropped her at a friend's house in Riverside. I stopped her right there. I asked her why she didn't get dropped off at my house. She told me she planned on being with her friend until Sunday and then she was coming to my house. She said she knew I wouldn't allow her to go anywhere or see anyone. She wanted to say hi and be with her family.

My wife was trying to calm me by patting me on the back. I calmly asked Sleepy why she was in jail. Sleepy said that at her friend's house they started drinking and smoking weed and meth. They partied all weekend then early Sunday morning they somehow pulled a woman out of her car and took off. (Somehow?) They drove around and then crashed the car. After the crash, Sleepy took off walking but had to stop because she had broken her nose in the crash. She was arrested a short time later for carjacking, under the influence of a controlled substance, great bodily injury, and various other charges.

I whispered to Sleepy, "You are going to prison." She answered, crying, "I know." I also whispered, "You lost your kids." She replied back, "I know." Her phone time was up and we said our goodbyes.

I spoke to Maria and Selena a short time later. They knew what had happened but were afraid to tell me. I was beside myself, I couldn't think straight. But the person I was the angriest at wasn't Sleepy. I expected her to act like an idiot. It was her dumb ass mother. She knew Sleepy was coming to my house to stay. She knew Sleepy shouldn't be dropped off in Riverside, especially at a homegirl's house, a friend who did drugs and belonged to the neighborhood gang. What the hell was she thinking? She should have just told Sleepy, "go back and do your drugs, mija." I was lost and I knew this was the last round.

I was afraid to share this new info with Jim. He wasn't surprised though. He just shook his head and was more concerned with the impact it had on me. He was a good friend and had helped me through all of the other incidents with Sleepy. I had prepared myself for something like this, I thought. I had always held on to the belief Sleepy would turn things around.

Every time I thought about Sleepy's kids, I had mixed emotions. I was happy they would hopefully be raised by good, responsible people. Anyone was an improvement over their biological parents. But I was sad because Sleepy's little boy was attached to her, they had bonded and I knew it would hurt him as it would hurt Sleepy, forever. I knew that if she could, Sleepy would turn back the hands of time and make things right. She had compassion and a good heart before the drugs changed that, leaving an ungrateful, selfish human being.

Inmate 65943, sit down and shut up. For the next three years in Chowchilla State Prison, that would be Sleepy's new name.

CHAPTER 23
A TASTE OF REALITY

Sleepy was transferred from city jail to state prison. All her actions and decisions had come to this. It had started so long ago, petty theft and being jumped into a gang, and all the other bad decisions. I guess it was inevitable. Staff at the prison, reading Sleepy's file would see a person who had been locked up off and on since she was a teen, the crimes committed, the placements, the group home, county jail time, the family history including a brother who served six years in prison, a dad overdosing on heroin, and Sleepy's last crime, the carjacking. What the file wouldn't show was the opportunities Sleepy had that she never took advantage of, the love and care and extra help shown by me, my family, the social workers, and others. The file also wouldn't tell of the family dysfunction. The reality of Sleepy's actions caught up to her and now she had to pay the piper.

3 Years Later:
Sleepy had almost completed her sentence of three years. We spoke occasionally and she would write letters when she could. She always begged me to put money on her books so she could buy things. She was up north in Chowchilla and once they had moved her to

Riverside. I went to see her there and ended up putting forty dollars on her books. It was the only time I did, I didn't really want to but I guess I was feeling generous, although she didn't deserve it.

Sleepy didn't have an easy time and would probably gotten out sooner but she had a fight and got into more trouble. When I did accept her calls, she would cry or be angry, but I would tell her, "That's where you wanted to be, so enjoy." When I would go up north to go fishing, she would get upset because she knew how much fun I had. Holidays were rough and she was depressed most of the time.

I would receive letters every once in a while. This is one she wrote in May, 2006:

As I toss and turn I sit here on my bed lost and unheard well surrounded by bob wire fences on a daily routine of how my program will be feeling trapped like the walls are closing in on me often times I want to hide and scream when reality falls I'm stuck in this place with nowhere to go in someone else's misery so as I continue to lay awake in the devil's playground I count my blessings for being alive striving to survive in this hell hole I hold my pride high and not cry though when weakness falls upon my heart I kick it up from falling apart and keep my shame sane for those I've caused pain for I'm the one to blame so I choke up the time I have left to spend in this place for I know I don't need to numb myself because even behind these walls and monitored gates I can still be free from the way I used to be when the devil was trying to sweep me so tonight I pray to the Lord that every night when darkness falls he would be the one I'll continue to call upon.

Sleepy

When I received letters like this, I would read them over and over again. It was like there was a hidden message she wanted me to see.

Another letter I received read like this:

Hey, what's up? As for me, I'm firme I guess, right here kicking back on my day off catching up on rest and taking time to get at you and tell you what's going on. Oh well, not much but trying to stay out of the mix and away from the drama of going to work and coming home to rest a little. I've been writing letters to my kids and going to the law library and making copies so I have track of them for myself. Well, I took the time to write Selena a letter too so I kept my word, right? I really miss that brat. I hope only the best for her. I want to see her make it out in the free world that is what she deserves. I'm trying to do what I can in here and at times I do get frustrated and feel like giving up on trying to be somebody but I can't continue to do that to myself let alone give much more action for my kids to have about me being such a failure and a bad mother and I want to change because I need to and I want to like I told Selena. I told Selena that I had it made and maybe didn't have all the material things but how long do material things last anyway. Yeah they can be cherish able and have special meanings behind them but we live without sometime, right? I know exactly how it is. What matters is doing what is right for me and trying to make amends to everyone I let down and hurt so much emotionally and verbally. It's awful when I think about it because I never meant it and in my right state of mind would I even have the right to come at anyone the way I did. I know I have a lot of anger inside for many different reasons. I didn't deserve not to have a bond with my mom and dad and a good relationship with them from my childhood. Now I am an adult and I must put it all behind me, right? I lost my dad already because there are no words to say to him now. I just pray things can get better between me and my mom before her time comes, you feel me, and put this all behind us. Well, there are a lot of things that can run through my mind all the time but a lot is helpful cause I can come to some understanding with myself and truths how both sides of life can be, and getting things together. Well, I'll talk to you soon, take care, and thanks so much, I appreciate everything you have done for me. OK, God Bless

> *The one and only*
> > *Youngster*
> *The kid*
> > *Sleepy*

P.S. can you please send me some stamps?

This letter told me a lot. First the prison lingo of "firme" which meant she was doing OK and then the "taking the time to get at you" which meant write a letter or talk to you. And calling prison "home"; second, so many thoughts going on about her dreams and desires and her relationship with her parents. Despite her problems and the dysfunction of her life and family, she still expressed her caring for Selena. She also recognized that she was a bad mother and had affected her kids and felt like a failure. She was trying to grasp all of it and had a hard time dealing with reality. Sleepy always knew what she needed to do but would never follow through with it. It was just too hard or too much for her to deal with. Her life was not easy and the burden of guilt pressed on her every day and night.

Sleepy was on the home stretch of her sentence. The phone rang one afternoon and Sleepy's parole officer asked if she could stop by and check out our residence. I was puzzled at first and then I figured it out. Sleepy had told the Parole Officer she would be living with us. I just laughed and told the officer that Sleepy wasn't and that it was a mistake. That little brat, I thought. Just wait till I talk to her. Sure enough, Sleepy called that night and I told her about my conversation with the Parole Officer. Sleepy asked me if I told her she wouldn't be living with us. I informed

Sleepy I wasn't going to lie to anyone for her. I have never lied for her and never would.

I wasn't surprised that she still had no qualms about lying and not wanting to walk the straight and narrow. She spent three years in prison but still hadn't managed to get her GED or diploma. I knew of kids who were in six month placements who were able to do it. Sleepy just blamed the prison system. It appeared that she didn't learn much in those three years.

There was a lot going on other than Sleepy's drama. Maria had been working at a major grocery store for over two years, and then she was fired. I knew she struggled to be on time and her phone calls to me had dwindled and then stopped, but I didn't know the extent of the problem. I found out she started smoking meth and wouldn't be home for days or weeks. Her mom called me to tell me that Maria was in bad shape and the school called every day because Maria's kids weren't attending. She was overwhelmed as usual and asked me for help. I told her to make the kids her first priority and to hell with Maria. Maria had had the most potential and I had been so proud of her. She had been the one out of the whole family that had a little stability. But she gave up and gave in and was in the process of losing everything. The other problem was that Sleepy was about to get out of prison and she was supposed to live with Maria. The whole purpose of Maria having a good job was to build her up and become stable so that she could help Sleepy when she was released. Now what?

Selena stumbled into troubled times too. When she got her DUI and was given weekends and classes, she only went to a few and never called her Probation Officer. There was a warrant out for her and I told her to take care of business because it wasn't going away. I was proud of her when she turned herself in, knowing she would probably do straight time. Her court date came and she was sentenced to one year at, guess where, Banning Road Camp, the same as Sleepy. What a family affair.

What a year it had been for this family. I was worn out just thinking about it. Sleepy was about to be released with nowhere to go, Maria was on drugs, and Selena was locked up in Banning. I remembered talking with them and their plans for the future, now their futures looked like hell. But there was no one to blame but themselves. Well I guess I picked the right family to give extra help too.

CHAPTER 24
RELEASE AND TRAGEDY

Prison time was over for Sleepy and Selena completed a year in Banning Road Camp. I spoke to Sleepy and we planned a day for her to come by the house and say hi. She sounded excited to be out and back with her family. A couple of days later she stopped by. When she walked up to the house, there were hugs and tears and smiles. We talked and talked, and she seemed to be the same old Sleepy as if three years had been three days. She was actually pleasant and was relieved and grateful to be free. Sleepy didn't know yet what she was going to do. She was staying with her sister. We talked about her years in the pen and she shared some scary stories and events that had happened. She survived, but had a rough time. I told Sleepy to help her sister, Maria and not be pulled in again to hitting the pipe. Sleepy gave hugs and well wishes and left. It was good to see her and my unconditional caring was confirmed.

Selena stopped by the house two days later. She seemed to have changed a little. She had always been this carefree, big smile kid, who even at 22 years old, looked like she was fifteen. She was famous for her cracking jokes. Selena had gained weight and aged a bit. She looked harder. She hadn't done well during her one year stint and had probably been beat up and abused. She being so petite and liking girls didn't help. Unfortunately, and it hurts to say this, but she had probably been someone's bitch while she was locked up.

Selena stayed for several hours. She had been dropped off in the morning and I was to take her home in the evening. She complained a little about my not sending her anything while she was locked up and how I only accepted a few of her calls. She wanted to know why I accepted more of Sleepy's calls. I told her that Sleepy had needed my calls and I was more disappointed in Sleepy. Selena just grinned a little as if to say "Oh yea."

Selena and I talked about her plans for the future. She sounded like she had things lined up but was just going to go with the flow, which is what she had always done. I dropped Selena off later that evening and gave her a few bucks.

It was so typical for Sleepy to spend one hour with us and Selena spent the whole day. It was just that way. In one weeks' time, one got out of prison and the other road camp. Crazy huh.

I drove home wondering what was going to happen to these two. I was pretty void of optimism at that point. They seemed to need drama in their lives, and they always found it.

Months would pass and I wouldn't hear from Sleepy. Selena would call from time to time and give me updates. None of her information was ever positive. She said Maria was jacked up on meth and not doing well. I told Selena that Sleepy was probably on the stuff too because she and her sister were so close. Selena said she wasn't sure about that. Selena also told me that all three of them were considering going to medical assistant school. I didn't know how serious they were about this, but I cheered them on anyway. We spoke for a while longer, I told her she was loved, and I hoped for more good news the next time we talked.

Selena said she was talking to my daughter on myspace the same time she was talking to me, so I said goodbye and left them to their younger conversation. My daughter loved Selena and knew Selena needed a friend to give her guidance and direction. My daughter did this and they were great friends. Selena loved my daughter back.

Two months passed and the three had started the medical assistant classes, but only two were still enrolled. Maria had attendance problems and was kicked out. Sleepy was at that point but was hanging on. Selena was attending and her behavior was good but she wasn't the student Sleepy and Maria seemed to be. Sleepy and Maria were not stupid, they could do the academics, but Selena struggled and had no self-confidence in school. Selena was only doing better because she was attending regularly. This is the way it stood for a while. They seemed to be just cruising along, going to school a little, hanging out, etc. Everyone else was taking care of Maria's kids because of the dope head she had turned into. Everything else seemed to be status quo until we checked the message machine.

I woke up at six o'clock as usual and started my morning routine. I made a pot of coffee and turned on my computer. I went outside for the morning paper and as I looked at my computer, I noticed the internet wouldn't come on. I tried several times but it still wouldn't work. I gave up and decided to read the paper front to back. My wife got up shortly after and I told her about the net not working. She checked the TV and the TV, phones and computer were all out. She called the service people and they said they couldn't be over until around noon. I wasn't too worried because I still had my cell phone. Later, the problem was fixed and my wife picked up the phone to check messages. She walked into the room with a look of pain and disbelief on her face. I asked her if everything was OK. She said she was sorry for the message that I must hear and she handed me the phone. I didn't even want to touch the phone; I wanted to run the other way. I knew it had to be bad. My wife lay down next to me on the bed, held me tightly, and told me again how sorry she was.

I pressed the button the phone and the message started. It was Sleepy and she was crying. She said Selena was at a friend's house and they had been drinking all night and at about 5:30 am she called Maria, upset and crying. Maria told her to go to bed and she would be there later to pick her up. Selena then called Sleepy and cried and said she wanted her mom. Sleepy spoke with her for a short time, but because of Selena's drunken state, Sleepy told her to go to bed and sleep it off. After her call to Sleepy, Selena went to her friend's garage, took an extension cord and hung herself. I dropped the phone and turned to hug my wife. I cried as if I had lost a daughter. I was confused and very angry. We stayed in bed holding each other.

Thoughts of Selena being twelve and working hard on her times tables flashed through my mind. I remember times in her teen years when she spoke about not wanting to live. We got through it though and I felt it was behind us. Some said she didn't really want to die. I don't know what I thought then, but I know what I think now. I am mad. I am angry. I am trying to comprehend this horrible act. It dawned on me, the morning everything went out and the phone didn't work, was the morning it happened. My phone didn't ring. My wife was quick to point out that Selena could have called my cell phone. But she did have to admit the timing was a bit odd.

I went through stages of pain and anger that day, then I started drinking and I lost it. My son had a baseball game and was the starting pitcher. I told him to pitch for Selena. My wife took him to the game and I stayed home. I drank away, and then my daughter, who hadn't heard the bad news, arrived home. She walked in and I was a mess. She started crying and demanded to know what had happened. I could barely speak but I managed to tell her about Selena. She cried even harder, and then she hugged me and stayed by me for the rest of the night.

My daughter was a much stronger person than I thought. She made me understand some things I hadn't thought about. She wouldn't allow me to blame myself and fought me with words when I made those comments. She was great that night, and I know she had her hands full. My wife and son returned home with the good news that my son had pitched six innings of a good game. At twelve years old, six innings is good. We all hugged and were thankful. We were just thankful for having each other.

It had been nearly three months since we heard the news about Selena. The family tried to bury her, but they didn't have the money, so they had her cremated. They tried to raise enough money by having car washes and other things but they fell short. It was no surprise that this family had no life insurance. They never asked me for money and I didn't offer. I was angry at Selena and as I told my wife; my money was for when she was alive. That may not have been the correct feeling but it was mine.

I still sit here months later and I am angry. I don't know if the feeling will ever go away. Selena's actions hurt me so badly and I will never forgive her for that. I will ask God to help me understand and also ask for direction, but only time will tell.

CHAPTER 25

A FINAL THOUGHT

I walked up to the house and out came Sleepy when she was just fourteen years old. This bagged pants, run downed face girl and her family would become one of the most important things in my life. The chaos of her family dysfunction and the impacts of all of their actions would change my life forever. I look back on all those years that had passed and I find myself leaning on what could have been. I attempted to beat the devil that I depicted as "street life." It has a hold on people and a desire to ruin lives by using drugs and gangs as a way to do it. I have always believed that a rose can grow in a bed of weeds. Through one's desires anything is possible and the outcome of anyone's life can be improved if one thing is done and it is done every minute of every day, CARE. Without caring, the devil and that street life are allowed to grab on and choke life away. As long as one cares, any challenge can be confronted and overcome.

I learned so much working with Sleepy and her family. If that's what God's wish was, then I accept it. I hope there is something more special in the future than this family being a teaching tool for me to learn and help others. The biggest thing I learned is that it boils down to the person and if and how they want to have a good life. I did everything I could think of to change the direction of this family's life. My wife and I even moved Sleepy and Selena in with us and now one is gone and the other is left with extreme challenges to this day. I find I am repeating myself to kids today. That I could move them into my house, try to improve their outlook on life, but they would still need to be the ones that have the desire to be something in this life. More importantly, they need to be the ones CARING.

I know there are many situations and challenges facing kids from all over the Country. I know many will identify with this family and may share some of the same problems Sleepy and her family have. I hope you use this story to better your life. My hope is that you wake up every day and build on CARING about yourself, more than you did the day before. I hope Sleepy inspires you to make better choices and to really see that the devil and "street life" are always looking for new victims. The ammunition that you must have to win is to CARE. If you do this, I promise your life will be better.

I spoke to Maria today. She told me that she was clean again and was hired full time at a clothing store. She said her mom was caring for her kids and she would get them back as soon as she got back on her feet. Maria told me that Sleepy had a new boyfriend and she stayed with him. She is staying out of trouble and is just getting by.

It is unknown to me the impact Selena's actions had on this family, I'm not around them anymore and I don't talk to them much. Maria did say everyone was doing better. I took that with a grain of salt. One thing is factual, Sleepy is still free. That's a good thing.

It was a Saturday and we were at home making tamales. We ran out of whole green chilis, so my wife asked me to run down to the market to buy some more. I drove down to the market wearing soft shorts and my slippers. I wasn't embarrassed even though I needed a shave too. I was walking down the center aisle and a girl in her early twenties was walking towards me, kind of staring at me. As I passed by her she whispered my name. I immediately stopped, now wishing I had cleaned myself up a little. She said, "It's me, Myra." I stood there stunned looking at this girl. She was beautiful and I noticed she was wearing the store's uniform. Myra was the oldest sister from a family just like Sleepy's that I had worked with years earlier. I spent three years trying to help out and one of her younger sisters. Myra's excitement at seeing me was overwhelming and her story of her life flew out of her mouth in seconds. She had worked at her job for four years, was buying a new car, and needed only one more semester for an AA degree. I was so proud of her; I hugged her several times. We exchanged phone numbers.

Myra had no idea about Sleepy and her family. She was an inspiration at a tough time. Myra is the perfect example of a person, who had every reason to give up, but she CARED and her hard work is paying off.

Sleepy, I love you. I hope that one day you CARE about yourself, others, and life.

Sleepy will be twenty five years old this year. Sleepy violated her parole and was sentenced to three more years in state prison. Her release date is April 11, 2012.

Selena donated her organs and gave three people she didn't know a second chance at life that she didn't give herself.

April 6, 2015

Sleepy,

I see you are a mother again. Your daughter is beautiful. It's good to see you off parole, working and looking healthy. Like most kids that get in trouble or lose their way, they all seem to have potential. You were no different. You had so much potential but the street life was tough and it almost cost you your life. I'm glad God gave you another chance and it looks like you are making the most of it. Stay strong thru the struggles it will surely bring. From CJ one more time- appreciate your freedom and value your life.

I never left your corner. I can finally say these words..
I'm proud of you......

Mike

DEDICATION

This book is dedicated to Sylvia Mendoza.

Sylvia, I remember the days when you were just 12 years old and you were learning your times tables. It was great to see you determined to learn them and also see you excited by the fact that if your score was high enough, the new taco from Taco Bell- CHALUPA would be your reward. We ate a lot of Chalupas now didn't we but guess what, it didn't take you that long to learn your times table.

You had a way about you that was indeed special. Your smile brightened a room and your loving heart will always be remembered. I'm glad we had our time and for someone who was already a father of three, you made me feel like I had another child. I know how much you cared about your family and my family and we will always remember you and always miss you.

Sometimes in life things happen and there is no turn- backs or try overs. I know you loved life and you were and always will be an inspiration to us all. At times I will walk in my living room and see your picture on my wall. I'll reminisce the ol days and smile as I remember you catching that trout, doing that dance or covering your enchiladas with sour cream.

I wish to see you again and have asked the lord to guide you, comfort you and watch over you. Until we meet again my dear

I love you

Mike

CPSIA information can be obtained
at www.ICGtesting.com
Printed in the USA
FSHW04n2025300318
46404FS